WJEC Eduqas
Poetry Anthology

If you feel like you need to brush up on your poetry skills, that's under-stanza-ble. Luckily, this CGP Poetry Guide explains it all — form, structure, language, themes, context... the lot.

We've included bags of brilliant online extras too. There's a free Online Edition, poem recordings and quizzes!

Unlock your free online extras!

Just go to **cgpbooks.co.uk/extras** and enter this code:

3086 8058 1759 1738

By the way, this code only works for one person. If somebody else has used this book before you, they might have already claimed the Online Edition.

GCSE English
The Poetry Guide

Contents

Contents

Section Four — Exam Advice

Section Five — How to Get a Top Grade

Section Six — Improving and Marking Sample Answers

You'll see **QR codes** on the Practice Question pages, which you can scan with any device. They'll take you to a set of **Sudden Fail Quizzes** for *The Poetry Anthology*.

There are separate quizzes for different themes — or you can try the **full quiz**, which combines the whole lot. Just scan the QR code to give it a go!

P.S. You can also find these quizzes at **cgpbooks.co.uk/eduqas-poetry/quiz**

Sudden Fail
Quiz

Where you see an **'Audio' stamp** like this, you'll find a **recording** of the poem online.

Just go to **cgpbooks.co.uk/extras** and enter the code at the front of this book.

Published by CGP

Editors:
Claire Boulter
Siân Butler
Heather Cowley
James Summersgill
Matt Topping

With thanks to Eleanor Claringbold for the proofreading.
With thanks to Emily Smith for the copyright research.

Acknowledgments:

Quote on the cover from 'The Prelude' by William Wordsworth.

'The Manhunt' by Simon Armitage from _The Not Dead_ (2008). Copyright © Simon Armitage

'Living Space' by Imtiaz Dharker from _Postcards from god_ (Bloodaxe Books, 1997)
Reproduced with permission of Bloodaxe Books. www.bloodaxebooks.com

'Cozy Apologia' from _AMERICAN SMOOTH_ by Rita Dove. Copyright © 2004 by Rita Dove. Used by permission of W.W. Norton & Company, Inc.

'Valentine' from _New Selected Poems_ by Carol Ann Duffy. Published by Picador. Copyright © Carol Ann Duffy.
Reproduced by permission of the author c/o Rogers, Coleridge & White Ltd., 20 Powis Mews, London W11 1JN

'Death of a Naturalist' by Seamus Heaney from _Death of a Naturalist._ Reprinted by permission of the publishers Faber and Faber Ltd.

'Hawk Roosting' by Ted Hughes from _Lupercal._ © Faber and Faber Ltd.

'Afternoons' by Philip Larkin from _The Whitsun Weddings._ © Faber and Faber Ltd.

'Dulce et Decorum Est' by Wilfred Owen from _Wilfred Owen: The War Poems_, edited by Jon Stallworthy (Chatto and Windus, 1994)

'Mametz Wood' by Owen Sheers. Published by Seren Press. Copyright © Owen Sheers.
Reproduced by permission of the author c/o Rogers, Coleridge & White Ltd., 20 Powis Mews, London W11 1JN

'As Imperceptibly as Grief' by Emily Dickinson from THE POEMS OF EMILY DICKINSON, edited by Thomas H. Johnson, Cambridge, Mass.:
The Belknap Press of Harvard University Press, Copyright © 1951, 1955 by the President and Fellows of Harvard College. Copyright © renewed
1979, 1983 by the President and Fellows of Harvard College. Copyright © 1914, 1918, 1919, 1924, 1929, 1930, 1932, 1935, 1937, 1942,
by Martha Dickinson Bianchi. Copyright © 1952, 1957, 1958, 1963, 1965, by Mary L. Hampson.

_Every effort has been made to locate copyright holders and obtain permission to reproduce sources. For those sources where it has been
difficult to trace the copyright holder of the work, we would be grateful for information. If any copyright holder would like us to make an
amendment to the acknowledgements, please notify us and we will gladly update the book at the next reprint. Thank you._

ISBN: 978 1 78294 363 1
Printed by Elanders Ltd, Newcastle upon Tyne.
Clipart from Corel®

Based on the classic CGP style created by Richard Parsons.

How To Use This Book

This book is for the Poetry Anthology section of the WJEC Eduqas GCSE English Literature exams.

You need to know the poems really well

1) For the **Poetry Anthology** section of your exam, you'll be given a **two-part question**. For the first part, you'll write about **one** poem **in detail**. The second part will ask you to choose **another poem** from the anthology and **compare** it to the first poem.

You can't take the poems or any notes into the exam, so you need to learn plenty of short quotes to use.

2) To write really good responses, you need to know all eighteen poems **in depth**. This book will help you to **understand** the poems and develop your ideas:

- **Section One** guides you through each poem in the anthology — read the **notes** on what each poem **means**, its main **features**, and the **attitudes** and **feelings** it conveys.
- Answer the **questions** about each poem — these will help you develop a **personal response** to it.
- When you feel confident that you know the poems **well**, have a go at the **questions** at the end of the section. They'll help you identify any **gaps** in your knowledge of the poems.

You'll have to write about the themes of the poems

1) In Section Two, the poems are grouped by **theme** to help you **understand** them better and to give you some ideas about which poems you could **compare** in the exam.

2) You can also use the summary of which **themes** relate to which **poems** inside the **back cover** to help you.

3) Then try the **practice questions** at the end of Section Two to check you're all up to speed.

Get to grips with the main features of each poem

1) Section Three is all about **form**, **structure** and **language**.

2) It looks at how the poets use techniques like rhyme and imagery to create **effects** — the examiners really want you to write about this.

3) There are some more practice questions at the end of the section to help you test your knowledge.

The code at the front of the book lets you access online extras to help you get to grips with the poems.

Tim got to grips with the 'self-destruct' feature of his brand-new car...

Learn how to write cracking exam answers

1) You need to know **how** to write great essays for your exam:

- **Section Four** gives you loads of **advice** on how to **plan** and **write** fantastic exam answers.
- There are several extracts from **sample answers** to show you the right way to approach the questions.
- **Section Five** is packed with **tips** on how to get a **grade 8-9** in the exam.

2) Once you know the **theory**, put it into **practice**:

- **Section Six** lets you test your skills by **adding quotes** or **extending points** to improve essay extracts. This will help you understand how to really **use the poems** to write **top-notch** answers.
- It also gives you some sample answers to **grade**, to help you see how to improve your **own answers**.

3) There's no substitute for getting some practice at **writing essays**:

- Use everything you've learnt to answer the **exam-style questions** at the end of Sections One to Three.
- You don't have to write a **full essay** for every question — making a **detailed plan** is still good practice.

The Manhunt

After the first phase,
after passionate nights and intimate days,

only then would he let me trace
the frozen river which ran through his face,

5   only then would he let me explore
the blown hinge of his lower jaw,

and handle and hold
the damaged, porcelain collar-bone,

and mind and attend
10   the fractured rudder of shoulder-blade,

and finger and thumb
the parachute silk of his punctured lung.

Only then could I bind the struts
and climb the rungs of his broken ribs,

15   and feel the hurt
of his grazed heart.

Skirting along,
only then could I picture the scan,

the foetus of metal beneath his chest
20   where the bullet had finally come to rest.

Then I widened the search,
traced the scarring back to its source

to a sweating, unexploded mine
buried deep in his mind, around which

25   every nerve in his body had tightened and closed.
Then, and only then, did I come close.

Annotations:

Repetition of phrases emphasises that the soldier's recovery is slow and painstaking.

Image of physical brokenness suggests that her husband struggles to talk about his experiences.

Repeated structure of two verbs in each stanza conveys the idea that she takes an active part in helping the soldier to get better.

A damaged parachute would be useless.

Comparing his ribs to the rungs of a ladder implies that his recovery is a slow, step-by-step process.

Double meaning of "grazed" — the bullet only 'grazed past' his heart, but it left emotional 'grazes' behind.

Image of a sweating bomb shows the tension and stress which his memories cause. He may not have dealt with some parts of his experience, as the mine is "unexploded".

His emotional injuries are hidden — it's difficult to get to this part of him.

Enjambment across stanzas gives the poem a sense of movement, reflecting the speaker's desire to keep making progress, even if it's slow.

The first couplet could be the start of a traditional love poem. It echoes the first stages of a new relationship and suggests the couple are reconnecting.

Full rhymes sound positive — they're making progress.

Images of the soldier's damaged body highlight how fragile he is. The fact that his body is broken down into a series of separate, broken objects suggests that war dehumanises people.

Personal pronoun shows the speaker is actively involved in her husband's recovery.

Figurative language suggests she's patching him up — it's as if she's tying his broken ribs back in place to make him strong again.

Half-rhyme could reflect that she's partially understood the link between his physical and emotional pain, but there's still a way to go.

Metaphor comparing the bullet to a foetus emphasises that his experiences are now a part of him. It could also hint that being injured is as life-changing as becoming a parent.

Extended metaphor — the speaker has found the source of the "river" from stanza 2. She's moving closer to the cause of his suffering, but it also shows he's not better.

The last lines don't fully rhyme, which makes this a muted ending — the speaker has made progress but can only "come close".

This is the only sentence that lies on one line. This gives emphasis to the wife's realisation that her husband's psychological 'scars' are worse than his physical ones.

Context — Effects of War on Soldiers

Although it isn't set in any particular time, the poem addresses common issues about the effects of war on soldiers' bodies and minds. It was originally aired as part of a television documentary, read by Laura, the wife of soldier Eddie Beddoes, who was injured while serving in the army. He suffered from depression and post-traumatic stress disorder (PTSD) as a result of his experiences. PTSD is a condition triggered by stressful or frightening events, and it affects many soldiers.

Glossary

parachute silk — material used for parachutes before the invention of nylon
struts — rods or bars designed to resist pressure and help maintain a framework's structure

Simon Armitage

Simon Armitage is an English poet, playwright and novelist. 'The Manhunt' is from his 2008 collection, *The Not Dead*, which looks at how war affects ex-soldiers, particularly those involved in recent conflicts.

You've got to know what the poem's about

1) The **wife of a soldier** gets to know her husband again after he returns home **injured** from war. The poem is sometimes subtitled 'Laura's Poem' — **Laura** (the soldier's wife) is the **speaker**.

2) Her husband has **physical** scars from the injuries he sustained in war.

3) He also has **psychological** 'scars' as a result of his **traumatic** experiences. The poem progresses from describing the scars on his **body** to exploring his **mental** 'scars' and how they **affect** him.

Learn about the form, structure and language

1) **FORM** — The poem's **couplet-long stanzas** have lines of **varying lengths**. Initially the couplets rhyme, but later on the rhymes **break down**, making the poem feel **disjointed** and reflecting the theme of **brokenness**.

2) **STRUCTURE** — Different **injuries** are introduced in different **couplets**, gradually moving **further** into the soldier's body. This allows the reader to **explore** his **body** and **mind** in the same slow process as his wife.

3) **LANGUAGE ABOUT THE BODY** — The soldier's body is presented using **adjectives** that describe **damage**. These are paired with **metaphors** that suggest his body has become a collection of **broken objects**. This could suggest that the damage has **taken away** some of his **humanity**, or these comparisons could be a way for his wife to **understand** and come to terms with his **injuries**.

4) **CARING LANGUAGE** — A range of different **verbs** is used to describe how the woman is **caring** for the injured man. Verbs like "<u>trace</u>" and "<u>attend</u>" are **gentle**, while "<u>bind</u>" shows how she is helping him to **regain his strength**. These words stress how **carefully** and **delicately** she cares for him.

Remember the feelings and attitudes in the poem

1) LOVE — The soldier's wife is sensitive in her approach to her wounded husband. She wants to help him and is slowly trying to get to know him again, in order to understand what he is going through.

2) PATIENCE — It takes the whole poem for the woman to just "come close" to her husband, and it's unclear how much more progress she will be able to make in the future. This shows how patient both the soldier and his wife will have to be for him to recover fully.

3) PAIN — The imagery in the poem suggests that the soldier suffers both physically and mentally. It's implied that his psychological trauma, rather than his physical pain, is the main cause of his suffering.

Go a step further and give a personal response

Have a go at answering these questions to help you come up with your own ideas about the poem:

Q1. Why do you think the poet called this poem 'The Manhunt'?

Q2. What impression does the reader get of the soldier's wife?

Q3. Do you think the end of the poem is hopeful? Explain your answer.

Effects of war, pain and suffering, love...

KEY THEMES 'The Soldier' and 'Dulce et Decorum Est' are about war too, but instead focus on the issue of soldiers dying in battle. You could also compare how a lover's body is shown here and in 'She Walks in Beauty'.

Sonnet 43

Enjambment emphasises the speaker's passion — it suggests she is overflowing with love.

Question makes the poem's theme clear from the start.

Addresses the object of her love as "thee" — it's direct and personal. However, the lack of a name or gender makes the poem seem universal.

The poem 'counts' each of these ways as it progresses. Makes the speaker sound methodical and intense.

Shows the scale of her love. Repetition of "and" reflects her excitement and passion.

This is a different side to her love — it's a calm, constant part of everyday life too.

She loves him effortlessly — it's very natural to her.

Anaphora shows the strength of her feelings. It also emphasises the different words that follow ("freely", "purely") which describe her love.

Capitals suggest these words are being used in a spiritual sense. The speaker's love is so deep it's like the desire to understand existence and get close to God. This would have resonated strongly with readers in the 19th century, when society was more religious.

She loves him as willingly as people who always try to do the right thing, and as purely as modest people who turn away from being praised. The link to virtuous conduct suggests her love is morally right.

> How do I love thee? Let me count the ways.
>   I love thee to the depth and breadth and height
>   My soul can reach, when feeling out of sight
> For the ends of Being and ideal Grace.
> 5 I love thee to the level of every day's
>   Most quiet need, by sun and candlelight.
>   I love thee freely, as men strive for Right;
> I love thee purely, as they turn from Praise.
> I love thee with the passion put to use
> 10 In my old griefs, and with my childhood's faith.
> I love thee with a love I seemed to lose
>   With my lost saints – I love thee with the breath,
> Smiles, tears, of all my life! – and, if God choose,
>   I shall but love thee better after death.

Mixture of positive and negative emotions shows that she loves him with everything she has — it all links back to her love for him.

She loves him with the passion that religion gave her as a child. This could suggest that her lover has replaced her faith — she almost idolises him.

Their love is presented as eternal as it will outlive their time on earth. The speaker's hope that God supports their love suggests that she believes in its purity.

Caesurae break up the rhythm and make her sound breathless with excitement.

Glossary

Grace — in Christianity, the love and mercy given by God to those who believe in him

Elizabeth Barrett Browning

Elizabeth Barrett Browning was born in County Durham. She wrote this poem as part of a series of sonnets published in 1850 about her future husband, Robert Browning, called *Sonnets from the Portuguese*.

You've got to know what the poem's about

Sonnet 44 — "I love thee more than doughnuts..."

1) The narrator expresses her **intense love** for her lover, counting all the **different ways** in which she loves him.

2) She loves him so **deeply** that she sees their love as **spiritual** and **sacred**.

3) Her love is so **great** that she believes she will love him even **after death**.

Learn about the form, structure and language

1) **FORM** — Barrett Browning follows **tradition** by writing her **love poem** in the form of a **Petrarchan sonnet**. This means it conforms to a **specific rhyme scheme**. It is written in **iambic pentameter**, and therefore mirrors the rhythm of **normal speech**, but the metre is disrupted by **pauses** and **repetition**, making the speaker sound **passionate**. The use of the **first person** also gives the poem a **personal** feel.

2) **STRUCTURE** — The poem is made up of a series of **different ways** of **defining** the speaker's love. The **octave** (the first eight lines) introduces the poem's main **theme** — the idea that her love is so intense, it is almost divine. The **sestet** (the remaining six lines) then develops this theme by showing that she loves him with the **emotions** of an **entire lifetime** — from **childhood** through to, and past, **death**.

3) **EXAGGERATED LANGUAGE** — The poem uses hyperbole to show the strength of the speaker's feelings. She uses exaggeration as she attempts to put her feelings into words — she is keen to emphasise both the scale of her love and the fact that the experiences of her whole life contribute to its strength.

4) **RELIGIOUS LANGUAGE** — The speaker's love is like a **religion** to her — it touches **all aspects** of her life and gives **meaning** to her existence. Her love is **unconditional**, like religious faith.

5) **REPETITION** — Using the same words repeatedly at the start of consecutive lines is called anaphora. It emphasises the strength of her feelings — it's as if words can't convey the intensity of her emotions, so she just has to keep repeating the same ones to express the depth of her love.

Remember the feelings and attitudes in the poem

1) DEEP AND LASTING LOVE — The speaker uses descriptions of spiritual love to emphasise the strength of her own feelings. The final line also implies that her love is everlasting.

2) UNSELFISH LOVE — The speaker asks for nothing in return. She compares herself to people who try to do the right thing without expecting a reward.

3) VIRTUE — She considers her love to be morally and spiritually right and worthy of God's support.

Go a step further and give a personal response

Have a go at **answering** these **questions** to help you come up with **your own ideas** about the poem:

Q1.   Why do you think the narrator hopes that her love is supported by God?

Q2.   What is the effect of the rhyme of "breath" and "death" in lines 12 and 14?

Q3.   The narrator focuses only on the positives of love in this poem. What is the effect of this?

KEY THEMES

Love and relationships, faith and worship...

'She Walks in Beauty' also uses exaggerated language to express strong feelings of love, while the poem 'Valentine' uses the metaphor of an onion to describe the positive *and* negative aspects of a relationship.

London

First-person narrator personalises the poem and makes it seem more real.

This sounds purposeless — it could reflect how he feels powerless to change what's happening.

Means 'notice', but also suggests everyone he sees is marked by experience.

Suggests the whole city is affected, not just one area.

Even powerful, natural features like the River Thames are under human control, and affected by the city's problems.

Repetition emphasises feeling of bleakness — despair affects everyone and there's no relief from it.

The speaker hears various distressing noises — makes this seem like a vivid, hellish experience.

People are trapped in every way, even by thoughts and attitudes.

Chimney sweeps were usually young boys — this is an emotive image of child labour.

Might be a reference to the French Revolution — sounds like he thinks ordinary people suffer while those in the palace are protected behind walls.

Seems to be angry at all forms of power — describing the church as "black'ning" could suggest that it is corrupt or that it is tarnished by its failure to look after people. It's also a grim visual image of the ugliness caused by the Industrial Revolution.

Contrast between innocence of youth and sordidness of prostitution.

He hears the prostitutes swearing, but he might also mean that they are a curse on London.

The innocence of newborn babies is lost immediately — society damages its members.

Powerful language of illness and disease. Destruction is implied by "blights", and "plagues" hints at something that's uncontrollable and destined to affect lots of people.

Oxymoron — links the happy image of marriage with death. Suggests that everything has been destroyed.

I wander thro' each charter'd street,
Near where the charter'd Thames does flow,
And mark in every face I meet
Marks of weakness, marks of woe.

5 In every cry of every Man,
In every Infant's cry of fear,
In every voice, in every ban,
The mind-forg'd manacles I hear.

How the Chimney-sweeper's cry
10 Every black'ning Church appalls;
And the hapless Soldier's sigh
Runs in blood down Palace walls.

But most thro' midnight streets I hear
How the youthful Harlot's curse
15 Blasts the new born Infant's tear,
And blights with plagues the Marriage hearse.

Context — 'Songs of Innocence and of Experience'

Blake wrote and illustrated two volumes of poetry which explored the state of the human soul. The 'Songs of Innocence' are positive poems which focus on childhood, nature and love, whereas the 'Songs of Experience' (including 'London') look at how that innocence is lost, and how society has been corrupted.

Glossary

charter'd — mapped out or legally defined
woe — sadness
ban — can mean either 'a curse' or 'to prohibit'
manacles — handcuffs
hapless — unfortunate
Harlot — a prostitute

William Blake

'London' was published in 1794. William Blake was an English poet and artist who held quite radical social and political views for the time — he believed in social and racial equality and questioned Church teachings.

You've got to know what the poem's about

1) The narrator is describing a **walk** around the city of London.

2) He says that **everywhere** he goes, the people he meets are affected by **misery** and **despair**.

3) This misery seems **relentless**. **No one** can escape it — not even the **young** and innocent.

4) People in **power** (like the Church, the monarchy and wealthy landowners) seem to be **behind** the problems, and do **nothing** to **help** the people in need.

Learn about the form, structure and language

1) **FORM** — This is a **dramatic monologue** — the first-person narrator speaks passionately and personally about the suffering he sees. The **ABAB** rhyme scheme is **unbroken** and seems to echo the **relentless** misery of the city. The regular **rhythm** could reflect the sound of his **feet** as he **trudges** around.

2) **STRUCTURE** — The narrator presents relentless images of downtrodden, deprived people. The first two stanzas focus on people he sees and hears, before a shift in stanza three to the institutions he holds responsible. The final stanza returns to look at people, showing how even newborn babies are affected.

3) **RHETORIC** — The narrator uses rhetorical language to persuade you of his point of view — he uses powerful, **emotive** words and images to **reinforce** the horror of the situation. **Repetition** is used to emphasise the **number** of people affected, and to show how society needs to **change**.

4) **USE OF THE SENSES** — The poem includes the depressing sights and sounds of a city — the first stanza shows what he **sees**, the second what he **hears**, and the last two stanzas combine the visual and aural.

5) **CONTRASTS** — These **show** how **everything** is affected and **nothing** pure or innocent remains.

Remember the feelings and attitudes in the poem

1) ANGER — **Emotive language** and **repetition** show the narrator's **anger** at the situation. He mentions "<u>Every black'ning church</u>" and "<u>Palace walls</u>", suggesting he's especially angry at the people in **power**, who could do something to **change** things but **don't**.

2) HOPELESSNESS — The "<u>mind-forg'd manacles</u>" suggest that the **people themselves** are also to blame — they're **trapped** by their own attitudes. They appear hopeless because they're not able (or not even trying) to help **themselves**.

Go a step further and give a personal response

Have a go at answering these questions to help you come up with your own ideas about the poem:

Q1.   Why do you think the poem is written in the first person?

Q2.   What is the effect of repetition in the poem?

Q3.   How would you describe the mood of the poem?

Q4.   What is the effect of setting the final stanza on "midnight streets"?

KEY THEMES

Negative emotions, sense of place, suffering...

'A Wife in London' uses images of the city to express an individual's feelings. You could also contrast the negative portrayal of a city here with positive images of the country in 'To Autumn' and 'The Prelude'.

8

The Soldier

Could mean that the land is literally English because of victory in war. It could also be meant figuratively — because his body will be buried there, a part of England will remain there.

First-person narrative voice is only apparent in the first line. This suggests that the poem could be about any soldier.

The narrator addresses the reader of the poem directly using an imperative — this makes the reader feel responsible for carrying out the soldier's request.

The soldier's body will remain in the field — the word "dust" has echoes of the phrase "ashes to ashes, dust to dust", from the 'Book of Common Prayer', which is commonly spoken at English burials.

'Richer' because of the body that lies there.

Repetition of words connected to England makes the narrator's love for his country seem overwhelming.

England is personified as a nurturing mother.

Nature is a positive force — it gives the soldier a sense of wellbeing.

Ending the stanza with this word emphasises the strength of the narrator's love for his country.

Commas slow the pace of the poem — this creates a more reflective mood.

The progression from "Gives" to "back" to "given" makes this line cyclical. This reflects the idea that in death, the soldier will give back the things England gave him in the first place.

Death is purifying and brings the soldier closer to "the eternal mind" — God.

Alliteration creates an echo effect which could reflect how these happy memories won't disappear — they'll be passed on.

The "heaven" will be "English" because the soldier thinks of England as a 'heaven'.

> If I should die, think only this of me:
>   That there's some corner of a foreign field
> That is for ever England. There shall be
>   In that rich earth a richer dust concealed;
> 5 A dust whom England bore, shaped, made aware,
>   Gave, once, her flowers to love, her ways to roam,
> A body of England's, breathing English air,
>   Washed by the rivers, blest by suns of home.
>
> And think, this heart, all evil shed away,
> 10   A pulse in the eternal mind, no less
>   Gives somewhere back the thoughts by England given;
> Her sights and sounds; dreams happy as her day;
> And laughter, learnt of friends; and gentleness,
>   In hearts at peace, under an English heaven.

Context — Idealism in World War One

When war was declared in August 1914, many men were eager to enlist to serve their country. 'The Soldier' captures this early idealism. However, as the war progressed and the true nature of war was realised, optimism began to fade. Some poets who experienced the war wrote realistically about its horrors — have a look at Wilfred Owen's 'Dulce et Decorum Est' on p.30-31.

Glossary

bore — gave birth to
blest — blessed

Rupert Brooke

The English poet Rupert Brooke wrote 'The Soldier' in 1914, the year World War One broke out.
He fell ill and died in 1915 while serving in the Royal Navy, and was buried on the Greek island of Skyros.

You've got to know what the poem's about

Jason's idea of heaven was
sunbathing on the beach
with a few friends.

1) The narrator, a soldier, is talking about the possibility of dying in a foreign country during war. He says that the area where he dies will be "for ever England".

2) He describes England as a mother who gave birth to him and raised him.

3) He believes that death will be comforting, and that he'll be able to give back the things that England gave him — his thoughts and memories won't be lost.

Learn about the form, structure and language

1) **FORM** — The poem is a **sonnet**, a form traditionally used for **love** poetry. Sonnets are usually written about another **person**, but here the object of the narrator's love is **England**. This **elevates** his emotions and shows how **strong** they are. The narrator appeals directly to the reader — his voice is **confident**, but becomes slightly more **reflective** in the second stanza.

2) **STRUCTURE** — In traditional sonnets, the **octave** (made up of eight lines) presents one idea and the **sestet** (made up of six lines) another. Brooke has followed convention in this poem — in the **octave**, the speaker shows how England has **enriched** his life, while in the **sestet**, he considers how, after his death, he will **return** the 'gifts' given to him by his country.

3) **PERSONIFICATION** — The poem uses an **extended metaphor** of England as a **mother**. This reflects how the speaker feels that his country has **shaped him** as a person. Mothers are often associated with **comfort**, which might explain why thinking about his country during a war seems to be **reassuring**.

4) **LANGUAGE OF NATURE** — The narrator talks about England's idyllic **nature** and **landscape**, including its "flowers" and "rivers". A love of the English countryside is part of his **devotion** to his **country**.

5) **RELIGIOUS LANGUAGE** — The speaker seems to be **religious** — he feels "blest" by England and refers to the "eternal mind" (God). The thought of "heaven" gives him **comfort** when he reflects on his death.

Remember the feelings and attitudes in the poem

1) PATRIOTISM — The narrator's **passion** for his **country** is clear — the first stanza contains a **long list** of all the things England has given him, while the second stanza lists the things he hopes to give back to England. This makes him seem **proud** to be English.

2) IDEALISM — The narrator's view of dying in war can be seen as **idealistic**. It doesn't reflect the **dirty, gruesome** and **painful** experiences of many soldiers during World War One. The poem might be a way for the narrator to **reassure** himself with the idea that part of him will **live on** when he dies.

Go a step further and give a personal response

Have a go at **answering** these **questions** to help you come up with **your own ideas** about the poem:

Q1.   What does "some corner of a foreign field" (line 2) suggest about the speaker's potential grave?

Q2.   What is the effect of England being compared to a woman?

Q3.   Do you think the poet is scared about dying? Why / why not?

KEY THEMES

Effects of war, nature, death and loss...

'Mametz Wood' is also about World War One and portrays the horrors of dying in war. You could write about 'A Wife in London', which shows how a soldier's plans for his life are thwarted by his early death.

She Walks in Beauty

Poem is narrated in present tense, making the woman's beauty seem eternal.

The narrator uses the extended simile of the night to describe the woman's appearance. He might be talking about the colour of her skin or hair, or the clothes she's wearing.

Imagery suggests the woman's beauty is pure. Alliteration highlights the contrast between dark and light — this woman represents the best of both.

The woman is the ideal mix of dark and bright things — the poem suggests that this is better than just being one or the other.

> She walks in beauty, like the night
>   Of cloudless climes and starry skies;
> And all that's best of dark and bright
>   Meet in her aspect and her eyes:
> 5   Thus mellowed to that tender light
>   Which Heaven to gaudy day denies.

Antithesis — the contrast between dark and light is enhanced by the line's balanced structure.

More imagery of light reinforces the idea that the woman is beautiful because she is a balance of the bright light of day and darkness.

Lots of verbs to do with movement and change — "walks", "waves" and "lightens". This makes the poem sound like a lively, real-time description, rather than a rose-tinted memory.

> One shade the more, one ray the less,
>   Had half impaired the nameless grace
> Which waves in every raven tress,
> 10   Or softly lightens o'er her face;
> Where thoughts serenely sweet express,
>   How pure, how dear their dwelling-place.

The adjective "nameless" suggests the woman is so beautiful it can't be put into words.

The woman's beauty shows that her mind — her thoughts' "dwelling-place" — is beautiful too. It's the first bit of information that isn't about her appearance.

Use of sibilance makes these lines sound soothing, just like her "sweet" thoughts and "soft" smiles.

> And on that cheek, and o'er that brow,
>   So soft, so calm, yet eloquent,
> 15   The smiles that win, the tints that glow,
>   But tell of days in goodness spent,
> A mind at peace with all below,
>   A heart whose love is innocent!

The narrator pays attention to different parts of the woman's face. This shows how attracted he is to her.

The words "mind" and "heart" are the first stressed syllables in these lines. The emphasis this gives them shows how much the narrator values these things.

Either innocent because she has never been in love, or because her love is virtuous and pure.

The narrator tells us that the woman has lived a moral life.

Context — Beauty and Nature

Many poets use nature to describe beauty. For example, Shakespeare does this in 'Sonnet 18', usually known by its first line "Shall I compare thee to a summer's day?" Byron uses nature differently to Shakespeare — he uses the night rather than the day to convey the woman's beauty.

Anya wasn't sure her tresses would elicit quite so much praise...

Glossary

climes — regions with a similar climate
aspect — appearance or face
gaudy — extravagantly, even tastelessly, bright
tress — a lock of hair
brow — forehead

Lord Byron

Byron (1788-1824) was a popular English poet, also known for his lavish lifestyle and scandalous affairs, although this poem is rather more restrained. Written in 1814, it was originally intended to be set to music.

You've got to know what the poem's about

1) The narrator describes a **woman** he's seen, taking her **individual body parts** in turn. He thinks she's incredibly **beautiful** and uses images of **dark** and **light** to emphasise how **perfect** she is.

2) He suggests that her **appearance** reflects her **personality** — she has spent her life doing **good things**.

Learn about the form, structure and language

1) **FORM** — The poem maintains a regular **ABABAB** rhyme scheme, reflecting the **enduring** nature of the woman's beauty and how she's a **balance** of different qualities. It's mostly in **iambic tetrameter** and uses a lot of **enjambment**, suggesting the narrator is **overwhelmed** by the woman's beauty.

2) **STRUCTURE** — The poem is split into **three stanzas** of equal length. As it progresses, the poem focuses less on the woman's **physical appearance** and more on her **inner beauty**. This could indicate that the narrator thinks that it is her **personality** that is most beautiful. However, his **evidence** that she is a moral person is her **beauty** — we don't know whether he knows her **properly**.

3) **CONTRASTS** — The poet employs **contrasts** to show how the woman is a **balance** of opposites, notably **light** and **dark**. He uses **antithesis** — where **contrasting** ideas are reinforced by a repeated structure — when he says that it would only take "<u>One shade</u>" more or "<u>one ray</u>" less to **reduce** her beauty.

4) **IMAGERY** — The imagery used in the poem, particularly that of the **night** and of **light and dark**, helps to express the narrator's view of the woman. For instance, the **purity** of the night sky reflects her **innocent** personality.

5) **LANGUAGE ABOUT THE BODY** — The narrator breaks the woman down into **individual body parts**. This shows how much he **admires** her, as he sees beauty in **all parts** of her. He seems to believe that her beauty is a **reflection** of her **morally good** character.

Remember the feelings and attitudes in the poem

1) **ADMIRATION** — The narrator is **amazed** by the woman and uses lots of different **images** and **techniques** to express her beauty. He loves how she is the **perfect balance** of different qualities and how her beauty reflects her **inner goodness**.

2) **ATTENTIVENESS** — The narrator thinks about the **different parts** of the woman's appearance and personality. He breaks down his description to look at each part of her **separately**. This emphasises the woman's **perfection**, as every part of her **deserves** his praise.

Go a step further and give a personal response

Have a go at **answering** these **questions** to help you come up with **your own ideas** about the poem:

Q1.   Why do you think the narrator uses the night instead of the day to describe the woman?

Q2.   Do you think the woman's mind or body is more important to the narrator? Why?

Q3.   How is nature important in the poem?

Love and relationships, worship...

Compare how love is expressed in other poems — in 'Cozy Apologia', the speaker talks humorously about her love for her husband, while 'Sonnet 43' uses religious language to describe feelings of love.

Living Space

Lack of "straight lines" in the building is highlighted by the ragged, uneven lines of the poem itself.

Matter-of-fact tone distances the narrator from the subject.

Tension between alliteration and enjambment. Alliteration holds the words together across the lines, giving the poem stability, while the enjambment creates instability.

"Nothing" is emphasised at the start of the line — this draws the reader's attention to the severity of the problem.

Long line juts out beyond the rest of the poem, mirroring the way parts of the building hang over each other.

The verb "thrust" is almost violent, creating a sense of danger.

Personification — the nails desperately "clutch" at the open space. They could symbolise the potential for a safer, more stable, structure.

The word "miraculous" is unexpected at the end of the stanza. In spite of all the disorder, there is still hope.

Title could suggest it's not a real 'home' — it's just a space for someone to exist in. However, it could also suggest that the space itself is "living" and therefore has the potential to change and develop.

Short stanza between two longer ones reflects how the inhabitant has "squeezed" a home into the structure.

Rhymes like "space" and "place" (lines 13 and 14) and "Beams" and "seams" (lines 5 and 8) link parts of the poem together — like the building, the poem is held together in places but lacks order.

The speaker reveals more emotion in this stanza. They are in awe that someone could live here.

Symbolism — eggs represent hope and the potential for a new or better life. However, they are also "fragile" and easily broken.

The "slanted universe" reminds us that the instability of this building is replicated on a larger scale. This could hint at the wider inequality in the world.

Hopeful "white" and "light" suggests there could be a better future ahead for the inhabitants, but "dark edge" might represent how hazardous and uncertain that future is.

Tension between the words "bright" and "thin" — there's hope but also fragility.

Here, the speaker is referring to the eggshells, but the use of the word "walls" makes the reader think about the building too. The fact that they are "walls of faith" suggests that the eggshells, the "living space" and faith are similar — they all involve optimism but are all breakable.

Stanzas 1 and 3 both end with references to faith — the inhabitants have faith that the structure is "miraculous" enough to be lived in, and that their eggs will be safe. The speaker might be suggesting that faith is what keeps people in difficult situations going.

There are just not enough
straight lines. That
is the problem.
Nothing is flat
or parallel. Beams
balance crookedly on supports
thrust off the vertical.
Nails clutch at open seams.
The whole structure leans dangerously
towards the miraculous.

Into this rough frame,
someone has squeezed
a living space

and even dared to place
these eggs in a wire basket,
fragile curves of white
hung out over the dark edge
of a slanted universe,
gathering the light
into themselves,
as if they were
the bright, thin walls of faith.

5

10

15

20

Imtiaz Dharker

Imtiaz Dharker was born in Pakistan, raised in Glasgow, and now lives in Britain and India. 'Living Space' comes from her 1997 collection, *Postcards from god*, and is about the housing in Mumbai, a city in India.

You've got to know what the poem's about

Barry was reluctant to put all his eggs in one basket...

1) The poem opens by **describing** a **building** — it's **badly built** and **falling apart**.

2) The speaker reveals that someone **lives** in the building, despite how **dangerous** it is.

3) The speaker notices there's a **basket of eggs** hanging outside. They describe how **fragile** the eggs are but also suggest that they represent some **hope** for the **future**.

Learn about the form, structure and language

1) **FORM** — The poem has an **irregular form**, using stanzas and lines of **different lengths**, mirroring the sense of **chaos** and **irregularity** in the building the speaker describes. The lack of regular rhyme and rhythm and the **enjambment** across lines and stanzas emphasise the **disorder** of the place. The final two stanzas are **one long sentence** — there's a growing sense of **wonder**.

2) **STRUCTURE** — The poem is split into **two parts**. It opens with a **description** of an unstable building. In the second and third stanzas, the **mood shifts** slightly, and the speaker begins to hint that there is **optimism** for the future, despite the **difficult circumstances**.

3) **LANGUAGE OF DISORDER** — The building's **chaos** is shown through words which suggest **instability**. For example, verbs like "<u>clutch</u>" emphasise the **danger** of the structure, but also make it seem **alive**.

4) **SYMBOLISM** — The **eggs** in the poem symbolise **faith** — the decision to place them outside requires the same sort of **courage** and **trust** as taking a leap of faith. However, the eggs are "<u>fragile</u>", which could suggest that faith can be 'broken' too. Eggs are often used to symbolise **new life**, which hints that the inhabitants have faith that the **future** (or possibly the lives of their children) might be **better**.

5) **LIGHT AND DARK** — The "<u>white</u>" eggs **stand out** against the "<u>dark edge</u>" which could represent the **dangerous** nature of the living conditions. The colour **white** is often associated with **innocence** — neither the **eggs** nor the **inhabitants** are to blame for the **precarious** situation they find themselves in.

Remember the feelings and attitudes in the poem

1) **DETACHMENT** — The poem opens with a **factual explanation** of the situation. The speaker describes the **physical features** of the building to show what the place is like without being **overly emotional**.

2) **AWE** — The speaker is **amazed** that someone could live here. Hanging the eggs outside is seen as a **defiant act** — someone has "<u>dared</u>" to place something fragile in a dangerous place.

3) **TENTATIVE HOPE** — **Optimism** for the future is presented through the **eggs** and the speaker's **admiration** for the space. The fact that the structure is "<u>living</u>" also means there's hope for **improvement**.

Go a step further and give a personal response

Have a go at answering these questions to help you come up with your own ideas about the poem:

Q1.   Why do you think the poem starts with a physical description of the building?

Q2.   Do you think the poet feels positively about the person living here? Why / why not?

Q3.   Is a solution to the problem included in the poem? Explain your answer.

Sense of place, faith...

Ideas of fragility are also present in war poetry, such as 'Dulce et Decorum Est' and 'The Manhunt'. Sense of place is another important theme in 'Living Space', and is also picked up in Blake's 'London'.

Section One — The Poems

As Imperceptibly as Grief

Poem's lines are generally short, giving the poem a sense of simplicity. This suggests a level of acceptance on the speaker's part.

The narrator establishes a link between summer and grief in the first two lines. This comparison holds throughout the poem — the surface message about summer represents the narrator's thoughts on grief.

Speaker seems sad that summer is over. It's not a betrayal ("Perfidy") but she doesn't welcome its end. The comparison in poem's opening lines hints that she feels the same way about grief.

Echoes the first line, emphasising the way that both summer and grief can slip away unnoticed.

Dashes slow down the pace of the poem — could reflect the slowness of the transition the speaker describes.

Summer and grief are associated with a sense of stillness and being closed off from the world. This is presented as comforting, rather than isolating.

The words "begun" and "Afternoon" only form a half-rhyme — could illustrate that the speaker isn't completely at peace with her feelings.

"Morning" symbolises the end of grief, but the fact it's "foreign" suggests that it feels strange to leave grief behind.

Light imagery highlights the cyclical nature of time. This links to the theme of death in the poem — life and death are part of this natural cycle.

Personification — "Morning" is like a guest who wants to leave. This suggests that everything has to come to an end, even if you don't want it to.

The "Morning" light is a "harrowing Grace" — suggests that something you expect to be pleasant can actually be unsettling.

As imperceptibly as Grief
The Summer lapsed away —
Too imperceptible at last
To seem like Perfidy —
5   A Quietness distilled
As Twilight long begun,
Or Nature spending with herself
Sequestered Afternoon —
The Dusk drew earlier in —
10 The Morning foreign shone —
A courteous, yet harrowing Grace,
As Guest, that would be gone —
And thus, without a Wing
Or service of a Keel
15 Our Summer made her light escape
Into the Beautiful.

Summer and grief leave us mysteriously (without the help of a "Wing" or "Keel"). Suggests their departure is a smoother transition than moving through air or water.

Transitions between the poem's natural metaphors are very gradual until "And thus" — it signals a shift in tone.

First-person plural "Our" includes the reader — suggests that the experience of something coming to an end is universal.

The "escape" of summer suggests that grief has also faded away. Summer escapes "Into the Beautiful", which hints that the end of grief is ultimately positive.

This is the only full stop in the poem. It's at the very end, which reflects the finality of summer (and grief) having passed. The last four lines have less punctuation than the rest of the poem, giving them a more decisive tone and suggesting the speaker accepts the change that has taken place.

Personification — summer's "escape" is an extended metaphor for what happens to the speaker's grief.

Glossary

imperceptible — so gradual that it's hard to detect
Perfidy — deceit, dishonesty
distilled — concentrated
Sequestered — hidden away
Keel — a piece of wood or metal which
helps a boat to balance in water

Emily Dickinson

Emily Dickinson was an American poet who was born in 1830. In her adult years, she lived in almost complete isolation but wrote many letters and poems. Her poems often discuss death and nature.

You've got to know what the poem's about

1) The poem begins by describing how summer comes to an end so gradually that you don't notice when it finishes.

2) The end of summer seems to represent the end of grief. The speaker suggests that the grieving process ends so subtly that it creates another sense of loss.

Sometimes it's more obvious when summer comes to an end...

Learn about the form, structure and language

1) **FORM** — The poem's rhythm mirrors the pattern of **everyday speech**, making it sound like the narrator's honest **thoughts**. The poet uses long dashes rather than conventional punctuation — these create **long pauses** and enhance the poem's slow, **reflective** mood.

2) **STRUCTURE** — The poem is a series of **natural metaphors** which reveal the speaker's feelings about the way that grief fades away **gradually**. The use of a **single stanza** adds to the sense of **gradual change** — there aren't any stanza breaks to split the ideas up. However, the speaker's **tone** becomes more **decisive** after line 13, which might reflect the way that she does **come to terms** with the fact that grief ends.

3) **LANGUAGE OF TIME** — The **passing of time** is a recurring theme in the poem — the changing of the **seasons** is associated with the **different stages** of grief. The fact that this association remains throughout the poem reflects the **slow**, almost **unnoticeable**, way that time **eases** the speaker's **grief**.

4) **LIGHT IMAGERY** — Images of natural light are present throughout. They remind the reader that the natural cycle of day and night will continue forever. This sense of inevitability could also be applied to other natural cycles, such as life and death, and perhaps also to grief and acceptance.

5) **CONTRADICTORY IMAGES** — The description of morning as "harrowing" and the comparison between summer (which is usually seen as pleasant) and grief are surprising. This could suggest that grief is not entirely unpleasant, and that its end involves contradictory emotions.

Remember the feelings and attitudes in the poem

1) **LOSS** — There are **various** types of loss in this poem: the loss of **summer**, the grief experienced after a **loved one's death** and then the **loss of grief** when it comes to an end. Both the loss of summer and the loss of grief take place **gradually** — the speaker **barely notices** the changes happening.

2) **COMFORT** — The speaker seems to find her grief **comforting** — perhaps because grief **connects** her to the person she has lost. There's a sense of **reluctance** in letting go and moving on, although the final **escape** of summer suggests that her grieving process **has to end**, and that this will ultimately be **positive**.

Go a step further and give a personal response

Have a go at **answering** these **questions** to help you come up with **your own ideas** about the poem:

Q1. What does the phrase "lapsed away" (line 2) suggest about the passage of time and grief?
Q2. What is the effect of describing the quietness as "distilled" (line 5)?
Q3. Do you think the overall feelings in the poem are happy or sad? Explain your answer.

Loss, passage of time, pain...

In 'To Autumn' and 'Afternoons', imagery of the seasons is also linked to the passing of time, while Hardy's poem 'A Wife in London' explores the theme of loss, specifically losing a loved one through war.

Cozy Apologia

Dedication to the poet's husband, Fred, makes it personal from the start.

—for Fred

Ordinary, domestic images contrast with imagery found in traditional love poetry.

Detailed, vivid image shows the importance of writing — it's part of the narrator's identity.

I could pick anything and think of you—
This lamp, the wind-still rain, the glossy blue
My pen exudes, drying matte, upon the page.
I could choose any hero, any cause or age

Stereotypical images of chivalry are used in quick succession. There's humour in her exaggeration.

5 And, sure as shooting arrows to the heart,
Astride a dappled mare, legs braced as far apart
As standing in silver stirrups will allow—
There you'll be, with furrowed brow
And chain mail glinting, to set me free:

Introduces the traditional cliché of the romantic hero and refers to Cupid's arrows. The speaker's tongue-in-cheek tone shows she isn't taking herself too seriously.

Sudden change of pace and subject — digressions give the poem a casual tone.

The speaker's partner is associated with freedom and safety.

10 One eye smiling, the other firm upon the enemy.

Hyphenation creates a sense of urgency which reflects modern communication.

This post-post-modern age is all business: compact disks
And faxes, a do-it-now-and-take-no-risks
Event. Today a hurricane is nudging up the coast,
Oddly male: Big Bad Floyd, who brings a host

Hurricane sounds gentle rather than dangerous.

Stanza 2 has lots of caesurae and enjambment. It creates a stop-start effect which mirrors the speaker's thought patterns.

15 Of daydreams: awkward reminiscences
Of teenage crushes on worthless boys
Whose only talent was to kiss you senseless.
They all had sissy names—Marcel, Percy, Dewey;
Were thin as licorice and as chewy,

Playful language shows she didn't take these relationships seriously.

Mocking the hurricane (they traditionally had female names). Humour undermines the danger.

Light-hearted extended metaphor shows that these relationships lacked substance.

20 Sweet with a dark and hollow center. Floyd's

Colloquial language makes the hurricane seem less dangerous.

Associated with safety and security.

Cussing up a storm. You're bunkered in your
Aerie, I'm perched in mine
(Twin desks, computers, hardwood floors):
We're content, but fall short of the Divine.

Ordinary details of their lives contrast with the clichés earlier in the poem.

Bird imagery links the couple together. This is emphasised by the word "Twin" in the next line.

25 Still, it's embarrassing, this happiness—
Who's satisfied simply with what's good for us,
When has the ordinary ever been news?
And yet, because nothing else will do
To keep me from melancholy (call it blues),

Adjective "content" emphasises that their love is ordinary but real. This contrasts with idealised love, which is often considered "Divine".

The speaker is self-aware, poking fun at their love — she's happy but sees the funny side of it.

Contrast between "melancholy", which sounds formal, and "blues", which is more colloquial.

30 I fill this stolen time with you.

Phrase is emphasised at the start of the line — it brings a change of tone which is stronger and more decisive.

Deliberate, final emphasis is on her partner.

Use of brackets makes the poem feel more personal and informal, as if we're hearing the speaker's thoughts as she's thinking them.

Context — Hurricane Floyd

In September 1999, the east coast of the United States was hit by Hurricane Floyd. Heavy rainfall caused extreme flooding and devastation.

Glossary

Apologia — a text written in defence of something
exudes — oozes out
Aerie — the nest of a bird of prey, usually built high up

Rita Dove

Rita Dove is an African-American poet. She won the Pulitzer Prize for Poetry in 1987 and in 1993, she became the US Poet Laureate. 'Cozy Apologia' was published in 2004 in the collection *American Smooth*.

You've got to know what the poem's about

1) As a **hurricane** approaches, the speaker takes **refuge** in her study and thinks about her partner.

2) She compares him to **everyday objects** as well as a **traditional knight** in shining armour.

3) She then reflects on a **range of topics**, such as modern life, the hurricane and old boyfriends, before returning to her **current relationship**. She says their love is **ordinary** but **genuine**.

Learn about the form, structure and language

1) **FORM** — The poem is written in **free verse**, which makes it sound **conversational**. The number of syllables in each line **varies**, creating the sense that 'Cozy Apologia' reflects the speaker's **train of thought**. The first stanza uses **regular rhyming couplets**, so the reader might expect that this is a **traditional love poem**. The rhyme scheme is **disrupted** in the middle of the second stanza, perhaps to reflect the **disorder** brought by the hurricane, but a **new ABAB** rhyme scheme is established in the final four lines.

2) **STRUCTURE** — The poem begins with a **personal description** of the speaker's feelings for her partner. She moves on to other topics but ends by describing their **ordinary**, **happy relationship**. The **hurricane** becomes important later on — the speaker's **thoughts** are mixed in with **references** to it.

3) **HUMOUR** — The speaker uses humour to prevent the poem becoming too **sentimental**. She does this by taking **exaggerated** or **clichéd images** of love and poking fun at them, while at the same time reinforcing her domestic, happy relationship. She doesn't take herself or her partner too **seriously**.

4) **EVERYDAY IMAGES OF LOVE** — By linking her partner to **domestic objects**, like a lamp or the ink on a page, the speaker emphasises that their relationship is **ordinary** — it's not an unrealistic image of love.

5) **COLLOQUIAL LANGUAGE** — Colloquial phrases make the poem seem **personal**. They contribute to the poem's humour and stop it from being **too serious**.

Remember the feelings and attitudes in the poem

1) **LOVE** — The poet uses imagery from the **ordinary** to the **clichéd** to describe her love for her partner. References to her "**worthless**" boyfriends of the past **contrast** with her current happy relationship.

2) **SAFETY** — The speaker feels **safe** and **protected**, rather than afraid, as the hurricane approaches.

3) **APOLOGY** — The title indicates that the poem is written in **defence** of her contented relationship. In the third stanza, the speaker suggests she's **embarrassed** by their love, but her happiness is **obvious** — she ends the poem by deciding that **focusing** on her lover is the most **worthwhile** thing to do.

Go a step further and give a personal response

Have a go at **answering** these **questions** to help you come up with **your own ideas** about the poem:

Q1. Why do you think Rita Dove called the poem 'Cozy Apologia'?

Q2. Find an example of enjambment. Explain why this technique is effective in this poem.

Q3. Do you think this is a romantic poem? Why / Why not?

Love and relationships, sense of place...

It's interesting to compare this poem with 'Sonnet 43', which uses exaggerated images of love to show the strength of the narrator's feelings. More unusual images of love are also used in 'Valentine'.

Valentine

Immediately clear that this is not a traditional love poem.

Personal pronouns highlight that this poem is for a specific person.

The moon is a traditional symbol of love and fertility.

The use of "It" makes it unclear whether the speaker means the onion or love itself.

The onion symbolises the way love can cause pain. Language like "blind" and "grief" is strongly negative, unlike traditional Valentine's Day messages.

Alliteration makes these seem overly sentimental and makes the narrator seem disdainful of them.

Echoes the wedding vow "For as long as we both shall live".

The offer of an onion in line 6 changes to a command. The speaker could be merely encouraging their lover to accept the gift, or their tone may be interpreted as confrontational, which makes the mood darker.

By placing "Lethal" alone on an end-stopped line, the speaker emphasises the idea that the onion symbolises danger and death. This is shocking and unexpected in a love poem.

Stereotypical symbols of love. The speaker implies these are clichéd and lack meaning.

Introduces the gift of an onion, which becomes an extended metaphor for love. It's an unexpected contrast with the first line.

This emphasises that the onion is a plain, unsentimental gift.

Hints at sexual love and physical intimacy.

Enjambment breaks these similes up, making the poem feel disjointed. The separation also emphasises how unpredictable the similes are — the comparisons don't necessarily end in the way the reader expects.

This line is unconnected to any others and almost divides the poem in two. It could represent the 'heart' of the poem — the speaker is trying to find the true meaning of love.

This repeated line presents the speaker as insistent and forceful, establishing a sense of unease.

Love is described in physical terms. There's also a suggestion that it can be dangerous and possessive.

Reference to a wedding ring could be a proposal. It's undermined by the sense of hesitation in the next line.

A powerful, disturbing final image. There's a hint that it refers to something more sinister than chopping an onion — but exactly what it could be is left unsaid. It implies that love has the power to wound.

The repetition of "cling" on two separate lines emphasises the inescapability of its "scent". The word also has a dark double meaning — it shows that love can be possessive and suffocating.

Not a red rose or a satin heart.

I give you an onion.
It is a moon wrapped in brown paper.
It promises light
5   like the careful undressing of love.

Here.
It will blind you with tears
like a lover.
It will make your reflection
10   a wobbling photo of grief.

I am trying to be truthful.

Not a cute card or a kissogram.

I give you an onion.
Its fierce kiss will stay on your lips,
15   possessive and faithful
as we are,
for as long as we are.

Take it.
Its platinum loops shrink to a wedding-ring,
20   if you like.
Lethal.
Its scent will cling to your fingers,
cling to your knife.

Carol Ann Duffy

Carol Ann Duffy is a Scottish poet who, in 2009, became the first woman to hold the post of Poet Laureate in the UK. 'Valentine' was originally published in 1993 as part of Duffy's collection, *Mean Time*.

You've got to know what the poem's about

"I give you some onions..."
"Urgh... no thanks."

1) The speaker of the poem is giving a gift to their partner. Rather than a traditional Valentine's gift, their gift is an onion.

2) The rest of the poem explains why the onion is a more appropriate symbol of love than other stereotypical gifts.

Learn about the form, structure and language

1) **FORM** — Duffy's poem is very different to traditional love poems. For instance, it is written in stanzas of irregular lengths, several of only one line, which makes the poem seem disjointed. Some lines are made up of single words, which gives emphasis to the forceful tone of the speaker.

2) **STRUCTURE** — The poem is a list of the ways the onion symbolises love. Words and ideas are built up and repeated throughout the poem. This could mirror the different layers of an onion, as the poem's meaning is revealed gradually. The tone is initially quite playful, but the speaker's repeated insistence that their partner accepts their gift could be read as either encouraging or confrontational.

3) **EXTENDED METAPHOR** — The extended metaphor of the onion is used to represent love. The speaker sees the onion as an honest symbol — it symbolises the joy and intimacy of love, but also the pain. It's an unusual metaphor, which contrasts with more stereotypical romantic symbols, like roses and cards.

4) **DIRECT ADDRESS** — The poem is written in the first person and directly addresses an unknown partner as "<u>you</u>" — it's very personal. The speaker uses commands like "<u>Take it</u>", which may be seen as forceful.

5) **DANGEROUS LANGUAGE** — There's an unusual amount of negative language for a love poem. Words like "<u>blind</u>", "<u>fierce</u>" and "<u>Lethal</u>" have a dark undertone. The speaker implies that this is a possessive relationship, while the word "<u>knife</u>" at the end hints that it might be dangerous.

Remember the feelings and attitudes in the poem

1) **LOVE** — The poet explores different forms of love. Love can be physical or emotional. It can be "<u>fierce</u>" and "<u>possessive</u>", and cause pain. There are also references to marriage and being faithful.

2) **HONESTY** — Above all, the speaker takes pride in being honest about love. She suggests that the traditional images of love, like red roses and cute cards, don't say anything real about love.

3) **DANGER** — At the end of the poem, there's a growing sense of danger, although it's only implied.

Go a step further and give a personal response

Have a go at answering these questions to help you come up with your own ideas about the poem:

Q1.   What does the word "platinum" (line 19) suggest about the onion?

Q2.   Do you think the poem describes a happy relationship? Explain your answer.

Q3.   How do you feel at the end of the poem? What do you think will happen next?

Love, relationships, negative emotions...

Think about the contrast between this poem and more conventional poems about love, such as 'She Walks in Beauty'. Other poems about relationships include 'The Manhunt' and 'Cozy Apologia'.

A Wife in London

The titles make the two halves of the poem seem like distinct acts in a play, or chapters in a novel. This first title sets up the expectation of bad news — there's a sense of inevitability.

The fog is yellow and thick — it's quite an eerie scene and there's a sense of foreboding. The word "webby" creates an image of a spider's web, suggesting the woman is trapped and her loss is inevitable.

The wife is presented as alone, against the backdrop of a bleak city.

I – The Tragedy

She sits in the tawny vapour
    That the City lanes have uprolled,
    Behind whose webby fold on fold
Like a waning taper
5   The street-lamp glimmers cold.

Onomatopoeia has a violent, harsh effect. It contrasts with the empty, silent scene in stanza 1.

The burnt-down candle foreshadows the way the husband's life is cut short.

Reference to a telegram delivering news.

There's no comfort or warmth in the street light — it adds to the anticipation of bad news.

A messenger's knock cracks smartly,
    Flashed news is in her hand
    Of meaning it dazes to understand
Though shaped so shortly:
10   He – has fallen – in the far South Land …

Dashes mimic the style of a telegram and create pauses, as if the news doesn't sink in.

Sibilance creates pace — it mirrors the urgency of the news.

Creates an uneasy mood.

The fog has got thicker, mirroring the wife's grief.

Caesura slows the pace down, as does the fact that the reader has to wait until stanza 4 to be told about the letter's contents.

II – The Irony

'Tis the morrow; the fog hangs thicker,
    The postman nears and goes:
    A letter is brought whose lines disclose
By the firelight flicker
15   His hand, whom the worm now knows:

Another image of light which echoes the street lamp from stanza 1. There's an inevitability in the repetition.

Another letter brings news — this structure mirrors the second stanza, creating suspense.

This vivid image is shocking. It highlights death and physical decay.

A morbid play on words, meaning both the husband's hand and his handwriting.

Fresh – firm – penned in highest feather –
    Page-full of his hoped return,
    And of home-planned jaunts by brake and burn
In the summer weather,
20   And of new love that they would learn.

Language of future plans and optimism creates a painful irony.

Pauses create a painful emphasis on the image of the husband as young and strong when he was alive.

Images of nature highlight the husband's youth and potential, which have been lost.

This is a final contrast between untimely death and new love. It emphasises the sense of irony.

Context — Communication during the Boer War

During the Boer War (1899-1902) in South Africa, news of a British soldier's death was sent by telegram, which was faster than normal post. Letters from the soldiers took longer to reach their families at home, as they were sent via normal post.

Glossary

tawny vapour — yellowish fog, which frequently covered London at the time
waning taper — a candle burning low
in highest feather — in high spirits
brake — bushes or bracken
burn — a small stream

Thomas Hardy

Thomas Hardy (1840-1928) was born in Dorset. 'A Wife in London' was written in 1899, during the time of the Boer War. Hardy was against the war — his poetry often presents war as pointless and destructive.

You've got to know what the poem's about

1) The poem opens with a description of a **wife** sitting at home in London. She receives a **telegram** with news that her husband, who has been at **war**, has been **killed**.

2) The next day, she receives a **letter** that her husband wrote before he died. In it, he says that he hopes he'll be coming **home** soon, and talks about his **plans** for their **future**.

Learn about the form, structure and language

1) **FORM** — The speaker in the poem is an **observer**. They use a **detached** tone, which presents the wife's grief as an **inevitable fact of war**. The **irregular rhythm** and **dashes** create pauses which force the reader to focus on the **tragedy**. The **asymmetrical** rhyme scheme (ABBAB) is **broken** only once — in the second stanza, the **half-rhyme** between "<u>smartly</u>" and "<u>shortly</u>" reflects the wife's **struggle** to take in the news.

2) **STRUCTURE** — The poem is clearly divided into **two parts**, each with its own **title**. The titles create **anticipation**, and the **factual descriptions** add to the speaker's **detached tone**. Images of light, e.g. "<u>glimmers cold</u>", and writing ("<u>**Flashed news**</u>") from the first half of the poem are **echoed** in the second half — this **repetition** emphasises how **similar** the situations are, but how they're fundamentally **different**.

3) **IMAGERY** — The detailed **visual** image of the fog **foreshadows** the wife's sorrow — it then "<u>hangs thicker</u>" when the bad news has been delivered. Images of light are presented as **lacking warmth** — the street lamp is "<u>cold</u>" and the candle is "<u>waning</u>". These could represent the **husband's life**, which has ended **too soon**, or reflect the **sadness** caused by his death.

4) **IRONY** — The title of the second half of the poem sets up the **expectation** of irony. Irony is created in the final stanza as the husband's **hopes** and youthful **energy** are **contrasted** with his wife's **grief**. This shows how the young man's **potential** and **future** have been cut short.

Remember the feelings and attitudes in the poem

1) **LOSS** — The wife's **grief** is anticipated from the start of the poem, and made more **poignant** by the **ironic arrival** of a letter from her husband, written before he died. Hardy uses the husband's death to highlight the **futility of war** — this young man was killed in his **prime**.

2) **HOPE** — The husband's letter is "<u>**Page-full**</u>" of his plans to return and the promise of "<u>**new love**</u>" together. There's a **youthful optimism** and **excitement** to his letter.

"OK, first one to the postman wins... On your marks..."

Go a step further and give a personal response

Have a go at **answering** these **questions** to help you come up with **your own ideas** about the poem:

Q1.   Based on this poem, how do you think the poet feels about war?

Q2.   What is the effect of the poem's setting?

Q3.   What do you think the words "new love" (line 20) could refer to at the end of the poem?

KEY THEMES

Death and loss, effects of war, love and relationships...

Ideas about loss are also explored in 'As Imperceptibly as Grief'. You could compare Hardy's poem with war poems, like 'The Soldier' or 'The Manhunt', to get a picture of different attitudes towards conflict.

Death of a Naturalist

Language associated with decay foreshadows the way the narrator becomes repulsed by nature.

Personification brings flax dam to life — reflects the narrator's fascination with nature.

Oxymoron shows childish enjoyment of something disgusting.

The sun is personified to make its heat seem oppressive.

Combined image of sound, touch and smell — it's a rich memory.

Sibilance mimics sound of flies buzzing.

Juxtaposition of beautiful creatures with disgusting slobber.

Introduction of childlike language and first-person voice show the narrator is slipping into their childhood self.

Usually describes a thick mass of something that used to be liquid — it's a powerful sensory image of the frogspawn.

Alliteration emphasises stickiness.

Use of simple conjunction "and" as well as a repetitive sentence structure convey the speaker's youth.

Enjambment emphasises the narrator's excitement.

The child narrator wants to share their interest with others.

Very short line makes the stanza end abruptly and signals the turning point (volta) in the poem.

Setting of stanza 2 echoes stanza 1 — emphasises that nature hasn't changed, just the speaker's opinion has.

Alliteration mimics the croaking.

Military language makes the frogs seem threatening.

Onomatopoeia makes the sounds stand out and seem more threatening.

Unusual simile compares their necks to huge sails, exaggerating the pulsing motion.

Simile suggests the frogs are about to explode — this shows how terrifying the speaker found them.

Personification — it's as if the frogs have authority over the narrator.

Shortest sentence in the poem emphasises the speed of the narrator's reaction. The list of verbs contrasts with the descriptive nature of the rest of the poem.

The poem ends with a nightmarish image — this reinforces how much the speaker's view has changed.

Narrator believes the frogs want revenge for taking the frogspawn.

All year the flax-dam festered in the heart
Of the townland; green and heavy headed
Flax had rotted there, weighted down by huge sods.
Daily it sweltered in the punishing sun.
5   Bubbles gargled delicately, bluebottles
Wove a strong gauze of sound around the smell.
There were dragon-flies, spotted butterflies,
But best of all was the warm thick slobber
Of frogspawn that grew like clotted water
10   In the shade of the banks. Here, every spring
I would fill jampotfuls of the jellied
Specks to range on window-sills at home,
On shelves at school, and wait and watch until
The fattening dots burst into nimble-
15   Swimming tadpoles. Miss Walls would tell us how
The daddy frog was called a bullfrog
And how he croaked and how the mammy frog
Laid hundreds of little eggs and this was
Frogspawn. You could tell the weather by frogs too
20   For they were yellow in the sun and brown
In rain.

    Then one hot day when fields were rank
With cowdung in the grass the angry frogs
Invaded the flax-dam; I ducked through hedges
25   To a coarse croaking that I had not heard
Before. The air was thick with a bass chorus.
Right down the dam gross-bellied frogs were cocked
On sods; their loose necks pulsed like sails. Some hopped:
The slap and plop were obscene threats. Some sat
30   Poised like mud grenades, their blunt heads farting.
I sickened, turned, and ran. The great slime kings
Were gathered there for vengeance and I knew
That if I dipped my hand the spawn would clutch it.

Glossary

Naturalist — someone who studies plants and animals
flax-dam — a place where bundles of flax (a plant) are put in water to be softened
sods — clumps of grass or pieces of turf
gauze — can mean a haze, or a thin piece of loosely woven fabric
bass — deep in pitch, usually referring to a voice

Seamus Heaney

Seamus Heaney was a Northern Irish poet who won the Nobel Prize for Literature in 1995 and died in 2013. He often wrote about themes such as childhood, nature and politics. This poem was published in 1966.

You've got to know what the poem's about

1) The narrator **remembers** how they used to collect frogspawn from a flax dam.

2) They were **enthusiastic** about **nature** and the sticky frogspawn. However, after the narrator **grew up**, they found the frogs **disgusting**.

3) The **shift** in the narrator's **perception** of **nature** highlights the way that **people's views** change as they grow up.

"Bow down to me, the Great Slime King!"

Learn about the form, structure and language

1) **FORM** — The poem has a **first-person narrator** who is reflecting on their childhood. It's written in **blank verse** (unrhymed verse), which makes the poem sound **conversational**. The lack of a **rhyme scheme** might suggest that change is **not always predictable**.

2) **STRUCTURE** — The poem has two stanzas, each one presenting a different attitude towards nature. Although there are references to decay in the first stanza, the narrator's childish enthusiasm makes their relationship with nature seem secure. There is a change in the second stanza, when this relationship becomes more troubled — nature is presented as unfamiliar and threatening.

3) **USE OF THE SENSES** — The poem contains language that appeals to the senses. The use of sensory imagery lets the reader become immersed in the poem and focuses their attention on the poem's setting.

4) **CONTRASTS** — The poem uses contrasts to show how the narrator's views on nature have changed. The juxtaposition in the poem's title shows that the poem is about both life and death — the speaker's interest in living creatures comes to an end.

5) **MILITARY LANGUAGE** — The second stanza is full of military references, which create a threatening atmosphere. This suggests that the narrator's innocence has been lost — they now see nature as something dark and potentially harmful.

Remember the feelings and attitudes in the poem

1) FASCINATION — The narrator was **interested** in the frogs and frogspawn. Their enthusiastic retelling of what they learned at school shows that they were a curious "<u>Naturalist</u>" as a child.

2) DISGUST — The language of **fear** and **repulsion** in the second stanza shows how the speaker's fascination has turned to **dread**. The **threatening** language used to describe the frogs contrasts with the **light-hearted** tone the speaker used earlier when talking about frogspawn.

Go a step further and give a personal response

Have a go at answering these questions to help you come up with your own ideas about the poem:

Q1.	Do you think the poem has a more serious or a more comic tone? Explain your answer.
Q2.	What is the effect of the repeated 'w' sound in line 13?
Q3.	What do the contrasting descriptions of frogspawn and frogs suggest about growing up?
Q4.	Why do you think Heaney mentions "Death" in the title?

Nature, change and transformation, sense of place...

'The Prelude' is similar to this poem, as it also has a first-person narrator who reflects on their youth and how their feelings towards nature have changed over time. In 'To Autumn', it's nature itself that changes.

Hawk Roosting

First-person narrator — hawk is controlling the poem.

The hawk is physically up high — symbolises its powerful position over the rest of nature.

Suggests the hawk is at peace because it knows it is so powerful that it doesn't have to fear anything.

Hawk's eloquence shows its mastery of language and emphasises its power.

Hawk's violence is emphasised as it thinks of killing even when asleep.

I sit in the top of the wood, my eyes closed.
Inaction, no falsifying dream
Between my hooked head and hooked feet:
Or in sleep rehearse perfect kills and eat.

Repetition highlights hawk's powerful features.

Only rhyming couplet in the poem. Emphasises how precise and perfect its kills are.

It sounds as if nature has been designed to suit the hawk.

The hawk looks down on everything, both literally and figuratively.

5   The convenience of the high trees!
The air's buoyancy and the sun's ray
Are of advantage to me;
And the earth's face upward for my inspection.

Exclamation shows hawk enjoys position of power.

Sounds sinister and tyrannical.

Pride — suggests that God had to work hard to create the hawk, but now nature and God are presented as tiny prey at the hawk's mercy.

My feet are locked upon the rough bark.
10   It took the whole of Creation
To produce my foot, my each feather:
Now I hold Creation in my foot

Harsh consonance emphasises hawk's tight grip.

Refers to "Creation" — ideas about power flow from one stanza to the next, reflecting how it's the hawk's dominant concern.

Oxymoron juxtaposes politeness with extreme violence to shock the reader.

Or fly up, and revolve it all slowly –
I kill where I please because it is all mine.
15   There is no sophistry in my body:
My manners are tearing off heads –

Simple, mainly monosyllabic language creates sense of control.

Dashes slow the pace of the poem — the hawk seems relaxed and confident.

Violent image of the hawk swooping in on its prey.

The allotment of death.
For the one path of my flight is direct
Through the bones of the living.
20   No arguments assert my right:

Ironic contrast between life and death — shows hawk's constant pursuit of killing things.

Double meaning of "behind me" — the hawk thinks the sun works with it, reinforcing its self-importance.

The sun is behind me.
Nothing has changed since I began.
My eye has permitted no change.
I am going to keep things like this.

Frequent use of negative statements suggests hawk is rejecting rules of society.

Emphasises the hawk's control — suggests it has had absolute power throughout its whole existence.

Parts of the hawk's body are addressed one by one throughout the poem — it's perfectly adapted to be powerful.

Framing device — beginning and ending poem with "I" reflects hawk's arrogance.

Creates a sense of certainty — the hawk believes it can keep the whole world as it is. This is ironic, as the reader knows it can't control everything.

End-stopping in final stanza gives statements a matter-of-fact tone.

Context — Different Interpretations of 'Hawk Roosting'

The poem caused some controversy when it was published. Some people thought it was an allegory for human nature. An allegory is a text in which characters or events represent real people or events, often to do with politics. They thought the hawk could symbolise a murderous tyrant who rules using violence and fear. However, Hughes has denied this and has explained that he intended the voice in the poem to be nature expressing itself.

Glossary

buoyancy — ability to float
sophistry — subtle false arguments used to deceive someone
allotment — the act of allocating something

Ted Hughes

Hughes (1930-1998) was born in West Yorkshire. In 1960, 'Hawk Roosting' was published. From 1984 until his death, he served as the British Poet Laureate, and he received the Order of Merit from the Queen.

You've got to know what the poem's about

1) The poem focuses on a hawk **boasting** about its power. The hawk thinks that it's the most **important** and **powerful** creature in the world and that it **controls** the universe.

2) The hawk describes how it likes to **kill** its prey in a particularly **violent** way.

3) People have interpreted the poem in **different ways** — it could be an **allegory** for the behaviour of **political leaders** or **people** in general, or it could be showing the **brutality of nature**.

Learn about the form, structure and language

1) FORM — This is a dramatic monologue from the point of view of a hawk. In a dramatic monologue, an individual character addresses a silent audience — in this poem, the audience could be mankind. The first-person narrative voice gives the hawk authority over the poem's ideas, while the use of end-stopping gives several lines a decisive feel, reflecting the hawk's complete control.

2) STRUCTURE — The poem begins with the hawk in an almost meditative state. The hawk then talks about God and nature, asserting that it has superiority over both of them. The monologue ends with a confident statement about the future — this emphasises the hawk's sense of power and control.

3) VIOLENT LANGUAGE — The poem contains powerful images of violence and death, which emphasise how efficiently the hawk kills its prey. The hawk almost seems to take delight in its ability to kill. It rejects subtlety and deception in favour of violent tactics.

4) LANGUAGE OF POWER — First-person pronouns appear in each stanza, establishing the hawk's dominance and control. It uses formal language, such as "sophistry", and political language like "my right". The hawk is presented as an articulate speaker, which emphasises how powerful it is.

Remember the feelings and attitudes in the poem

1) **POWER** — The poet presents the hawk as powerful and **destructive**. Its power has been **unchallenged** and it's confident that nothing will change. However, since the hawk is a part of **nature**, it will inevitably lose its power when it **dies**. The fact that the hawk **doesn't** seem to know this could suggest that it **isn't as powerful** as it thinks.

2) ARROGANCE — The hawk's attitude is **egotistical** and arrogant — it believes that it is **superior** to both nature and God. It's unclear whether its **confidence** is **legitimate** or not.

Go a step further and give a personal response

Have a go at answering these questions to help you come up with your own ideas about the poem:

Q1.   How does the poet create a sense of the hawk's superiority?

Q2.   Why do you think Hughes chose a poetic form without a rhyme scheme for this poem?

Q3.   Do you agree with the hawk's opinion of itself? Explain your answer.

Q4.   How might the hawk's nature reflect human nature?

Nature, death, negative emotions...

Shelley's 'Ozymandias' also includes ideas about pride and arrogance. The theme of nature is explored in 'To Autumn' and 'The Prelude', while 'Death of a Naturalist' looks at nature's threatening side too.

To Autumn

Narrator directly addresses autumn.

Soothing alliteration makes autumn seem gentle.

Exclamation mark hints at narrator's awe.

Connects autumn with the morning — the sun has risen and is getting higher in the sky.

The word "bosom-friend" already implies closeness, so "Close" isn't needed. It exaggerates the closeness, reflecting the overflowing abundance in this stanza.

Humans and nature are interlinked.

Poem is rich with adjectives and details — mimics the abundance of autumn.

Symbolism — fruit represents life.

There's a hint of sadness — this is the first indication that winter is coming.

Suggests they're ripe almost to the point of bursting.

Negative connotations — summer has provided too much.

Season of mists and mellow fruitfulness!
 Close bosom-friend of the maturing sun;
Conspiring with him how to load and bless
 With fruit the vines that round the thatch-eaves run;
5 To bend with apples the moss'd cottage-trees,
 And fill all fruit with ripeness to the core;
  To swell the gourd, and plump the hazel shells
 With a sweet kernel; to set budding more,
And still more, later flowers for the bees,
10 Until they think warm days will never cease,
  For Summer has o'erbrimm'd their clammy cells.

Ambiguous — could mean either carefree or showing a lack of care.

Autumn is personified and is directly addressed by the narrator.

Words related to human industry show that autumn provides for humans.

Consecutive rhetorical questions make the speaker sound scornful of spring.

Each stanza is made up of two parts — the first line is one and the remaining lines form the other. The second part is a very long sentence, which reflects the idea of abundance.

The hook used for cutting and the word "Spares" evoke images of the grim reaper (death personified), which hints at the decay winter brings.

Repetition of "hours" makes the line sound sluggish, reflecting the slow passage of time.

Who hath not seen thee oft amid thy store?
 Sometimes whoever seeks abroad may find
Thee sitting careless on a granary floor,
 Thy hair soft-lifted by the winnowing wind;
15 Or on a half-reap'd furrow sound asleep,
 Drows'd with the fume of poppies, while thy hook
  Spares the next swath and all its twined flowers;
And sometimes like a gleaner thou dost keep
20 Steady thy laden head across a brook;
 Or by a cyder-press, with patient look,
  Thou watchest the last oozings hours by hours.

Speaker reassures themselves and autumn.

Evocative image of a reaped field — autumn is coming to an end.

Lambs born in spring are bigger now — reflects the passing of time.

Autumn has multiple personas — farmer, brewer, singer. Shows the abundance the season brings.

This contrasts with the long summer days mentioned earlier.

Contrasting images of life and death suggest the narrator has mixed emotions.

The lambs' bleating shows that, even though winter is coming, the natural world is still rich with life.

Where are the songs of Spring? Ay, where are they?
 Think not of them, thou hast thy music too, —
25 While barred clouds bloom the soft-dying day,
 And touch the stubble-plains with rosy hue;
Then in a wailful choir the small gnats mourn
 Among the river sallows, borne aloft
  Or sinking as the light wind lives or dies;
30 And full-grown lambs loud bleat from hilly bourn;
 Hedge-crickets sing; and now with treble soft
 The red-breast whistles from a garden-croft;
 And gathering swallows twitter in the skies.

The robin symbolises the coming of winter.

Swallows migrate south for winter — their gathering represents the end of the year. Migration isn't permanent, so it also symbolises hope that there will be new life again.

Glossary

bosom-friend — old-fashioned word for close friend
thatch-eaves — the part of a thatched roof which hangs over the wall of the building
gourd — a fruit of the pumpkin or squash plant
kernel — the edible part of a nut
cells — the chambers that make up bees' honeycomb
winnowing — blowing air through grain to remove the bits that humans can't digest

furrow — a long, narrow trench created by a plough
swath — a line of a crop as it lies when reaped
gleaner — someone whose job it is to collect fallen grain
sallows — willow trees
bourn — can mean either a boundary, or a small stream
treble — a high-pitched singing voice

John Keats

John Keats (1795-1821) was an English Romantic poet. Near the end of his life, he contracted tuberculosis, causing his health to deteriorate quickly. In 1820, Keats published six odes, one of which was 'To Autumn'.

You've got to know what the poem's about

1) The narrator directly addresses autumn, which is personified throughout.
2) The poem begins by describing the plentiful nature of the start of autumn — there's an abundance of produce. It then moves on to describe the work that people do during the harvest, and the final stanza reflects on the passage of time as autumn fades and winter approaches.

Learn about the form, structure and language

1) **FORM** — 'To Autumn' is an ode, a serious poem that is usually written in praise of a person or thing. It's written in iambic pentameter, but its rhyme scheme changes slightly. The first four lines of each stanza always have an ABAB pattern but the rest of the second and third stanzas is different to the first. Keats's other odes have ten lines per stanza — this one has eleven, reinforcing the plentiful nature of autumn.

2) **STRUCTURE** — In each stanza, Keats introduces an aspect of autumn in the first line, before expanding on it in the remaining ten lines. The poem's structure can be seen as showing the passage of time — the first stanza links morning with early autumn, the sleepy mood in the second could stand for mid-autumn and the afternoon, and the final stanza hints at both the approach of winter and sunset.

3) **LANGUAGE OF EXCESS** — Language to do with abundance shows how autumn can produce a bountiful harvest. However, the harvest is just beyond the point of perfection — the speaker hints that it's too much. The language of excess could therefore symbolise the start of death.

4) **PERSONIFICATION** — The speaker personifies autumn in the second stanza and shows that it's hardworking but also takes breaks and relaxes. Autumn ages throughout the poem in the same way a human does — this seems to be mourned in the final stanza.

5) **SENSORY LANGUAGE** — Each stanza appeals to a different sense — the first focuses on the sense of touch, the second on sight, and the last on sound. This reflects the abundance of autumn — it is present all around. Many of the poem's images are described in detail, underlining the richness of the season.

Remember the feelings and attitudes in the poem

1) **AWE** — The narrator admires the power of nature, taking delight in its beauty and abundance.
2) **SORROW** — There is a slightly sad tone as the narrator senses that autumn also signifies the start of winter.

Go a step further and give a personal response

Have a go at answering these questions to help you come up with your own ideas about the poem:

Q1.   How does the mood of the poem change as it progresses?

Q2.   What does the word "bend" (line 5) suggest about the apples on the trees?

Q3.   Why do you think the poet chose to personify autumn? Explain your answer.

Q4.   Why do you think Keats wrote this poem in the form of an ode?

Nature, passage of time, death...

Have a look at the way 'As Imperceptibly as Grief' explores the passage of time and compare it to how it is discussed in this poem. The theme of nature is explored in 'Death of a Naturalist' and 'The Prelude'.

Afternoons

Change in seasons mirrors a change in people's lives. It suggests that the people in the poem have peaked and now their lives are "fading".

Makes change seem irregular and uncontrollable.

The word "hollows" suggests their daily routine is empty. The fact that "afternoons" is plural suggests that this emptiness applies to all afternoons.

Enjambment puts the focus on the recreation ground. The word "new" and the 'creation' part of "recreation" are ironic as they imply change, but the people's routines remain the same.

Women are only referred to as "mothers", which implies they're restricted by gender stereotypes.

Sibilance creates a sense of repetition, hinting that this happens regularly.

Caesura emphasises the separation between the women and their husbands.

Language of imprisonment suggests domestic life is restrictive.

Suggests the people in the poem are working-class.

Women are anonymous — they have no individuality.

Focus on the letters makes the words themselves seem meaningless.

Groups the people of the estate together — makes the narrator seem dismissive of them.

Implies their love has become something ordinary and neglected.

Quoting the name of the album in italics makes the speaker sound patronising.

Suggests their opportunities are being taken away by something they can't control.

"Behind them" and "Before them" in lines 9 and 15 highlight the separation between the women and their previous identities as "lovers". The fact that their "courting-places" are being ruined "Before them" hints that this is a permanent change.

Enjambment over the stanza break, coupled with repetition of "courting-places", suggests that even though the "lovers" change, their lives still follow the same pattern.

The word "Expect" is emphasised at the start of the line — suggests the children are restricted by routine. Could also hint that the children's expectations contribute to their mothers' restricted lives.

End-stopping in line 22 makes the last two lines feel separate from the rest of the poem. It also makes the reader think about what the "Something" is.

This is the only standalone sentence in the poem — emphasises how the change in tense connects their past and present.

Summer is fading:
The leaves fall in ones and twos
From trees bordering
The new recreation ground.
5 In the hollows of afternoons
Young mothers assemble
At swing and sandpit
Setting free their children.

Behind them, at intervals,
10 Stand husbands in skilled trades,
An estateful of washing,
And the albums, lettered
Our Wedding, lying
Near the television:
15 Before them, the wind
Is ruining their courting-places

That are still courting-places
(But the lovers are all in school),
And their children, so intent on
20 Finding more unripe acorns,
Expect to be taken home.
Their beauty has thickened.
Something is pushing them
To the side of their own lives.

Context — 1960s Britain

In the 1960s, when this poem was published, society was quite different to how it is now. Gender roles were more defined then — women were expected to dedicate themselves to raising children and looking after the home, while men were typically expected to have a job and provide for the family. In addition, the government was taking steps to get rid of old, run-down housing and replace it with new, modern estates with plenty of green spaces.

Philip Larkin

Philip Larkin (1922-1985) was born in Coventry. 'Afternoons' was published in 1964 as part of the collection called *The Whitsun Weddings*. Much of his poetry explores the ordinary events that occur in people's lives.

You've got to know what the poem's about

1) The poem is very **observational**. The narrator describes an **ordinary scene** — children play while their "<u>Young mothers</u>" stand by.

2) The narrator paints a **picture** of the women's restricted lives for the reader, describing **routine chores** such as laundry and **ordinary objects** such as televisions.

3) The poems ends by showing that the women's **lives** have **changed**, and now they are no longer in **control** of their own lives. There's a sense that the **next generation** will follow the **same pattern**.

"I've no idea why the kids ran away screaming..."

Learn about the form, structure and language

1) **FORM** — The poem is split into **three equal stanzas**. There's **no regular metre**, which makes the poem feel **stilted**, suggesting a **lack** of excitement in the mothers' lives. The poem is narrated in the **third person**, but the **tone** is **unclear** — the speaker could be **belittling** the women or **pitying** them.

2) **STRUCTURE** — The speaker establishes the setting first, then focuses on the women's lives, starting with their **present** and then examining their **past identities** as young "<u>lovers</u>" — this allows the reader to **contrast** what the women's lives were like with what they're like now. The final stanza returns to the present and implies that nothing will change and that there's no hope for the future.

3) **GENERALISATIONS** — The speaker uses specific **objects**, such as wedding albums, to make **sweeping statements** about **working-class women** and their lives.

4) **DOMESTIC IMAGERY** — The narrator's images of domestic life reinforce the gender roles of the era, which appear to be the cause of the women's repetitive existences. The images also show how the marriages have lost their spark over time and how love has settled into something ordinary.

5) **NATURAL IMAGERY** — Nature is used to mirror **change** in people's lives. The arrival of autumn suggests that a **new phase** of the women's lives has started and the **best** part is **over**. The way that the wind ruins their "<u>courting-places</u>" makes it seem as though nature is actively **working against** them.

Remember the feelings and attitudes in the poem

1) SYMPATHY — The speaker's **word choice** and **imagery** (e.g. "<u>hollows</u>" and "<u>estateful of washing</u>") convey the **monotony** of the women's lives, which may suggest that the speaker feels sympathy for them.

2) SUPERIORITY — The speaker's **tone** seems to mock the women at times, for example by describing their **beauty** as "<u>thickened</u>" and belittling the title of the **wedding album**.

Go a step further and give a personal response

Have a go at **answering** these **questions** to help you come up with **your own ideas** about the poem:

Q1.   What does the title suggest about the stage the women in the poem are at in their lives?

Q2.   Why do you think Larkin made the speaker's tone unclear? Explain your answer.

Q3.   What does the verb "assemble" (line 6) suggest about the women's lives?

Change, love and relationships, passage of time...

'Cozy Apologia' also uses domestic imagery to discuss relationships, but in a more positive way than in 'Afternoons'. You could look at Lord Byron's 'She Walks in Beauty', which discusses women and love.

Dulce et Decorum Est

Implies the soldiers have been physically broken by war.

Similes show how the soldiers have been affected by war — "old" suggests they've lost their youth, while "hags" takes away their masculinity.

Metaphor emphasises their exhaustion and inability to function properly.

Caesurae slow the pace of the poem, emphasising how slowly the soldiers are walking.

Repetition and exclamation marks create a sudden change of pace.

Simile draws out the soldier's painful death.

These lines feel linked to stanza 2 because they continue the rhyme scheme, but their detachment from it makes the poem feel deformed, reflecting the way the soldiers have been damaged by war.

Repetition of "all" emphasises the widespread suffering.

Ironic as it suggests excitement when actually the soldiers are panicking.

Implies the soldiers were ill-prepared.

Stanzas 2 and 4 use long sentences to emphasise how vivid the narrator's memories are.

Repetition of "drowning" and the fact that it's rhymed with itself emphasises that the image is stuck in the speaker's mind.

Using '-ing' verbs emphasises that the actions feel immediate and inescapable for the narrator.

Alliteration draws attention to the injured soldier's movement and the pain he suffered.

The words "devil's" and "sin" have connotations of evil. This imagery dehumanises the soldier — war takes away his humanity.

Graphic similes intensify the dying soldier's suffering.

The narrator appeals to the reader's sense of sound to try to help them understand the reality of war.

Emphasises the soldiers' innocence.

The capital 'L' suggests that the "Lie" is well-established.

Vivid descriptions present the physical horrors of war.

Ironic tone reveals that the narrator disagrees with people who say it's noble to die for your country.

Latin makes this phrase sound prestigious and traditional. However, the last line is unexpectedly short, which could suggest that the attitude behind the phrase is responsible for soldiers' lives ending abruptly. The use of Latin could also suggest that people don't fully understand what they'll face if they fight for their country.

Bent double, like old beggars under sacks,
Knock-kneed, coughing like hags, we cursed through sludge,
Till on the haunting flares we turned our backs
And towards our distant rest began to trudge.
5   Men marched asleep. Many had lost their boots
But limped on, blood-shod. All went lame; all blind;
Drunk with fatigue; deaf even to the hoots
Of gas shells dropping softly behind.

Gas! GAS! Quick, boys! — An ecstasy of fumbling,
10   Fitting the clumsy helmets just in time;
But someone still was yelling out and stumbling,
And flound'ring like a man in fire or lime ...
Dim, through the misty panes and thick green light,
As under a green sea, I saw him drowning.

15   In all my dreams, before my helpless sight,
He plunges at me, guttering, choking, drowning.

If in some smothering dreams you too could pace
Behind the wagon that we flung him in,
And watch the white eyes writhing in his face,
20   His hanging face, like a devil's sick of sin;
If you could hear, at every jolt, the blood
Come gargling from the froth-corrupted lungs,
Obscene as cancer, bitter as the cud
Of vile, incurable sores on innocent tongues, —
25   My friend, you would not tell with such high zest
To children ardent for some desperate glory,
The old Lie: Dulce et decorum est
Pro patria mori.

Context — Use of Chlorine Gas in World War One

Chlorine gas was a weapon used by both sides during the war, which was fought from 1914 to 1918. It was a distinctive shade of green and when inhaled, it caused breathing difficulties, and eventually death.

Glossary

lime — short for quicklime, a substance that can burn human skin
cud — food that cows digest partly, then chew again
ardent — very keen or enthusiastic
Dulce et decorum est / Pro patria mori — a Latin phrase that means "It is sweet and proper to die for your country"

Wilfred Owen

Wilfred Owen was a soldier in World War One, and he wrote 'Dulce et Decorum Est' during the war. It was published in 1920, after his death. Much of Owen's poetry reveals his anger at the war's horrific conditions.

You've got to know what the poem's about

1) The poem describes the suffering of exhausted soldiers marching away from battle.

2) Suddenly, the soldiers are attacked with chlorine gas, and the narrator sees a man die. He's haunted by this image in his dreams.

3) The narrator paints a graphic picture of the soldier's injuries and uses his experiences to warn against telling people that fighting for their country is honourable.

Learn about the form, structure and language

1) **FORM** — The poem uses **alternate rhymes** (ABAB etc.) which reflect the **relentlessness** of the soldiers' suffering. However, **enjambment** and **caesurae** create a disjointed rhythm and a variable pace. The **irregular stanza length** and **metre** add to the sense of **uncertainty**, reflecting war's **unpredictable** nature.

2) **STRUCTURE** — The **tone** of the poem is **serious** at the start as the narrator paints a picture of his **memories** of war, and later explains how they still affect him in the **present**. The poem then becomes an **appeal** aimed directly at the reader, and the narrator adopts an **ironic tone** to put his **opinion** across.

3) **REALISTIC IMAGES OF WAR** — The poem opens with images of the **reality** faced by soldiers at war — they are "<u>Knock-kneed</u>", "<u>blood-shod</u>" and "<u>lame</u>". These realistic images show the **effect** that war has had on the soldiers — they're **injured**, possibly in **life-changing** ways.

4) **GRAPHIC IMAGERY** — As the poem progresses, the narrator's descriptions become more graphic — the imagery is particularly disturbing in the final stanza. This shocks the reader and aims to remove the honour that some associate with fighting for their country by showing people the horrific reality of war.

5) **USE OF SOUNDS** — The narrator appeals to the reader's sense of sound to allow them to understand the horrors of war. Sounds in the final stanza such as the blood "<u>gargling</u>" are contrasted ironically with the first stanza, where the soldiers are "<u>deaf</u>" due to their exhaustion.

Remember the feelings and attitudes in the poem

1) SUFFERING — The narrator portrays the exhaustion that the soldiers experience, as well as the real risk of dying a painful death. As the poem progresses, the narrator also touches on the way he continues to suffer emotionally after the event.

2) CRITICISM — The speaker wants to dismiss the idea that fighting for your country will bring honour and glory. He contrasts the horrific reality of war with the "<u>old Lie</u>" that it's honourable to go to war.

Go a step further and give a personal response

Have a go at answering these questions to help you come up with your own ideas about the poem:

Q1.   What does the phrase "smothering dreams" (line 17) suggest about the effects of war?

Q2.   Why do you think Owen chose the title he did? Do you think it's an effective title?

Q3.   Why does the poet only start to address the reader in the final stanza? Explain your answer.

Effects of war, pain and suffering, death and loss...

Compare how suffering is examined in this poem to how 'The Manhunt' explores the ways that soldiers suffer after a war. You could also look at how dying in war is handled in this poem and in 'The Soldier'.

Ozymandias

Shelley frames the poem as a story to make it clear that the narrator hasn't even seen the statue himself, he's only heard about it. This emphasises how unimportant Ozymandias is now.

Emphasises size and stature but also shows that the statue is incomplete.

The setting suggests an absence of life and vitality.

The sculptor understood the arrogance of the ruler.

'Mock' can mean to ridicule, or to create a likeness of something — perhaps the sculptor intended his statue to make fun of Ozymandias.

Having a stressed syllable at the start of the line heightens Ozymandias's tone of command.

Ironic — even a powerful human can't control the damaging effects of time.

Having "survive" and "lifeless" on the same line hints at how art can outlast human power, but the ruined statue shows that ultimately art can't immortalise power.

Arrogant and powerful — he even challenged other rulers.

Irony — he tells other rulers to "despair" because of the size and grandeur of his "works", but in fact they should despair because their power is temporary and ultimately unimportant, like his.

I met a traveller from an antique land
Who said: Two vast and trunkless legs of stone
Stand in the desert ... Near them, on the sand,
Half sunk, a shattered visage lies, whose frown,
5   And wrinkled lip, and sneer of cold command,
Tell that its sculptor well those passions read
Which yet survive, stamped on these lifeless things,
The hand that mocked them, and the heart that fed:
And on the pedestal these words appear:
10 'My name is Ozymandias, king of kings:
Look on my works, ye Mighty, and despair!'
Nothing beside remains. Round the decay
Of that colossal wreck, boundless and bare
The lone and level sands stretch far away.

The ruined statue shows how human achievements are insignificant compared to the passing of time.

Alliteration — emphasises the feeling of empty space in the surrounding desert.

The desert is vast and survives far longer than the broken statue, emphasising the insignificance of the statue and of Ozymandias.

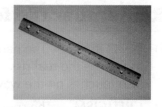

This ruler was nowhere near as powerful as Ozymandias...

Context — Shelley

Shelley was a Romantic poet — Romanticism (see p.53) was a movement that had a big influence on art and literature in the late 1700s and early 1800s. Romantic poets believed in emotion rather than reason, tried to capture intense experiences in their work and particularly focused on the power of nature. Shelley also disliked monarchies, absolute power and the oppression of ordinary people. His radical political views were inspired by the events of the French Revolution, where the monarchy was overthrown.

Glossary

Ozymandias — another name for Ramesses II, a ruler of Ancient Egypt
antique — ancient
trunkless — without a torso
visage — face
pedestal — base of a statue
colossal — very large

Percy Bysshe Shelley

Percy Bysshe Shelley was a Romantic poet, who only really became famous after his death. He wrote 'Ozymandias' in 1817, after hearing about how an Italian explorer had retrieved the statue from the desert.

You've got to know what the poem's about

1) The narrator meets a **traveller** who tells him about a **statue** standing in the middle of the desert.

2) It's a statue of a **king** who ruled over a past civilisation. His face is **proud** and he arrogantly **boasts** about how **powerful** he is in an **inscription** on the statue's base.

3) However, the statue has fallen down and **crumbled away** so that only the ruins remain.

Learn about the form, structure and language

1) **FORM** — The poem is a **sonnet**, with a **turning point** (volta) at line 9 like a **Petrarchan** sonnet. However, it doesn't follow a regular sonnet rhyme scheme, perhaps reflecting the way that **human power** and structures can be **destroyed**. It uses **iambic pentameter**, but this is also often **disrupted**. The story is a **second-hand account**, which **distances** the reader even further from the dead king.

2) **STRUCTURE** — The narrator builds up an image of the statue by focusing on **different parts** of it in turn. The poem ends by describing the **enormous desert**, which helps to sum up the statue's **insignificance**.

3) **IRONY** — There's **nothing** left to show for the ruler's arrogant boasting or his great civilisation. The ruined statue can be seen as a **symbol** for the temporary nature of **political power** or human **achievement**. Shelley's use of irony reflects his **hatred** of **oppression** and his belief that it is possible to **overturn** social and political **order**.

4) **LANGUAGE OF POWER** — The poem focuses on the power of Ozymandias, representing human power. However his power has been **lost** and is only visible due to the power of **art**. Ultimately, **nature** has **ruined** the statue, showing that **nature** and **time** have more **power** than anything else.

5) **ANGRY LANGUAGE** — The **tyranny** of the ruler is suggested through **aggressive** language.

Remember the feelings and attitudes in the poem

1) PRIDE — The ruler was **proud** of what he'd achieved. He called on other rulers to **admire** what he did.

2) ARROGANCE — The inscription shows that the ruler **believed** that he was the most powerful ruler in the land — nobody else could **compete** with him. He also thought he was **better** than those he ruled.

3) POWER — Human civilisations and achievements are **insignificant** compared to the passing of **time**. **Art** has the power to **preserve** elements of human existence, but it is also only **temporary**.

Go a step further and give a personal response

Have a go at **answering** these **questions** to help you come up with **your own ideas** about the poem:

Q1.   Why do you think the poem is set in a vague "antique" land?

Q2.   Why do you think "Nothing beside remains" comes directly after the ruler's proud inscription?

Q3.   What does the poem suggest about the way Ozymandias ruled?

Q4.   How might Romanticism have influenced the tone of the poem?

KEY THEMES

Nature, passage of time, negative emotions...

You could compare how the relationship between humans and nature is explored in this poem and in 'The Prelude'. Hughes's 'Hawk Roosting' is about a proud hawk and is written from its point of view.

Mametz Wood

Image suggests nursing something wounded.

Refers both to the decaying bodies and to the lives that were lost too soon.

The soldiers are unidentified and nameless — war has taken away their individuality.

The earth can recover after being damaged by war, unlike the dead soldiers.

A relic is an old object and also a part of a saint's body that gets worshipped — could suggest admiration for those who died.

The soldier's shoulder blade is compared to a fragile, everyday object. This dehumanises him and suggests he is easily broken.

Caesurae split the body parts up — implies that death takes away the soldiers' identities.

Alliteration contrasts the violence of war with the fragility of the skull.

Time shifts forward, showing how long the healing process takes.

This is disturbing as "nesting" implies new life — suggests weapons are part of nature.

Simile continues personification of earth being injured.

Personification suggests the earth preserves their bones in a determined but calm way.

Beauty of mosaic contrasts with the image of broken bones.

Comparing soldiers to a "foreign body" emphasises that they shouldn't be there — it's unnatural that they've died so young.

Image of skeletons dancing creates dark humour, but also reminds us of the soldiers as living beings.

Turning point (volta) — poem shifts from earth to talking about bodies of soldiers.

Suggests they were shouting or their mouths were open in horror.

Vivid and disturbing image reminds reader that they have decayed.

Parenthesis reminds the reader of the soldiers' injuries.

Creates a gentle image — the poem ends with a sense of peace.

Discovering the soldiers gives them a voice that they've lacked.

Continues bird imagery from stanza 2. The human image of the soldiers in song also contrasts with the violence of war.

For years afterwards the farmers found them –
the wasted young, turning up under their plough blades
as they tended the land back into itself.

A chit of bone, the china plate of a shoulder blade,
5   the relic of a finger, the blown
and broken bird's egg of a skull,

all mimicked now in flint, breaking blue in white
across this field where they were told to walk, not run,
towards the wood and its nesting machine guns.

10 And even now the earth stands sentinel,
reaching back into itself for reminders of what happened
like a wound working a foreign body to the surface of the skin.

This morning, twenty men buried in one long grave,
a broken mosaic of bone linked arm in arm,
15 their skeletons paused mid dance-macabre

in boots that outlasted them,
their socketed heads tilted back at an angle
and their jaws, those that have them, dropped open.

As if the notes they had sung
20 have only now, with this unearthing,
slipped from their absent tongues.

Context — The Battle of the Somme

The Battle of the Somme was fought between July and November 1916 during World War One. As part of the battle, some Welsh soldiers were commanded to walk towards the Germans with the aim of capturing Mametz Wood. However, the soldiers came under fire and there were many fatalities. Even though the attack was successful, some people criticised the Welsh soldiers for showing a lack of determination. Others felt that the soldiers had been badly treated — they felt the soldiers had been badly trained and that and their sacrifice had not been appreciated.

Glossary

Mametz Wood — a real place in the Somme region of France which was the scene of an intense battle during World War One
stands sentinel — stands guard
dance-macabre — an idea common in medieval art and literature where Death leads people to the grave

Owen Sheers

Sheers was born in 1974 in Fiji but grew up in Abergavenny in South Wales. 'Mametz Wood' is about a battle fought in France during World War One. It was published in the collection *Skirrid Hill* in 2005.

You've got to know what the poem's about

1) The poem begins with **farmers** in France in the present finding **bones** and **skeletons** in their fields when they plough the land. The skeletons and bones are from **soldiers** who died during **World War One**.

2) The poem briefly references the way the soldiers **died** in battle before returning to the grisly **discovery** of their skeletons in the present.

3) This discovery is partly **positive** — it allows the **memory** of these soldiers to be **honoured**.

Learn about the form, structure and language

1) **FORM** — The poem is written in **tercets** (3-line stanzas). It's written in the **third person**, which creates a sense of **distance** and **detachment**. Long sentences and enjambment establish a **reflective** tone.

2) **STRUCTURE** — The poem moves forward **chronologically** and in the fifth stanza, the poet describes finding a **mass grave** that morning. The thoughtful tone and slow pace **don't change** and images of the **past** are there all through the poem. This emphasises the **lasting effects** of war and the **time** it takes for the earth to heal.

3) **PERSONIFICATION** — The **earth** is personified both as someone who needs **healing** and as someone guarding the soldiers' **memory**. This emphasises how **long** it takes to **recover** from the **damage** war causes and also stresses the **importance** of **remembering** those who fought in the war.

4) **IMAGES OF BROKENNESS** — The narrator details **injured body parts** in a list in the second stanza and later describes the **damage** to the skeletons. It shows how war can **dehumanise** people.

5) **CONTRASTING IMAGES** — The narrator often contrasts **violent images** of war with **images of human fragility**. It reminds the reader of the soldiers' **humanity** and the **horrifying conditions** they faced.

Remember the feelings and attitudes in the poem

1) SADNESS — The **mournful**, lyrical tone suggests a **calm sadness** for the deaths of the young soldiers.

2) HORROR — The horror of their death is **understated**, which makes it feel **distant**. It is **implied** by small details — even the **grotesque** images of the linked skeletons are presented using a **gentle** tone.

3) REMEMBRANCE — In the poem, **nature** seems to be making sure that the dead soldiers aren't **forgotten**. There's a strong sense that **memory** is important and that the **past** shouldn't be forgotten.

Go a step further and give a personal response

Have a go at answering these questions to help you come up with your own ideas about the poem:

Q1. What impression does the narrator give of how the soldiers died?

Q2. What is the effect of the repetition of "back into itself" in lines 3 and 11?

Q3. How is the rural landscape important in the poem?

Q4. What is the effect of the narrator's detached tone?

Effects of war, nature, death...

'Dulce et Decorum Est' is also about the effects of war and the horror that soldiers face. You could also compare the descriptions of soldiers' bones in this poem with the burial described in 'The Soldier'.

Excerpt from 'The Prelude'

> The narrator sets up a wintry scene for the reader.

> The narrator rebels by not going home, showing his youthful enthusiasm and excitement.

> The bright lights of the cottage echo the setting sun, creating a sense of light and warmth.

> Starting the line with "Proud" highlights the narrator's confident and carefree attitude.

> Caesurae create pauses mid-line, suggesting the narrator is breathless and excited.

> Sibilant sounds mimic the sound of ice skates.

> Emphasises that the narrator is fast, energetic and excitable.

> Children's game compared to hunting, suggesting they're wild and energetic.

> Simile associates the narrator with strength, youthful energy and nature.

> Turning point (volta) signals a shift in focus from people to nature — nature is set apart from humans.

> Suggests speed and energy in their movements.

> The sounds of the humans are loud, familiar and boisterous.

> Sibilance reflects how nature is echoing the children's sounds back at them.

> The word "alien" emphasises how the sound of nature contrasts with the familiar noise of the happy children.

> Double negative suggests that humans do notice the sounds of nature but don't fully understand them.

And in the frosty season, when the sun
Was set, and visible for many a mile
The cottage windows through the twilight blaz'd,
I heeded not the summons: – happy time
It was, indeed, for all of us; to me   5
It was a time of rapture: clear and loud
The village clock toll'd six; I wheel'd about,
Proud and exulting, like an untir'd horse,
That cares not for his home. – All shod with steel,
We hiss'd along the polish'd ice, in games   10
Confederate, imitative of the chace
And woodland pleasures, the resounding horn,
The Pack loud bellowing, and the hunted hare.
So through the darkness and the cold we flew,
And not a voice was idle; with the din,   15
Meanwhile, the precipices rang aloud,
The leafless trees, and every icy crag
Tinkled like iron, while the distant hills
Into the tumult sent an alien sound
Of melancholy, not unnoticed, while the stars,   20
Eastward, were sparkling clear, and in the west
The orange sky of evening died away.

> Onomatopoeia of "Tinkled" is softer than the human sounds, and suggests nature's sounds are otherworldly.

> Enjambment places emphasis on "melancholy", which highlights a contrast with the narrator's feelings earlier in the poem.

> Multiple caesurae slow down the pace and make these lines more reflective.

Context — 'The Prelude'

This is an excerpt from the first of fourteen books that make up Wordsworth's poem, 'The Prelude'. The book is entitled 'Introduction — Childhood and School-Time'. Wordsworth was a Romantic poet (see p.53). Like other Romantic poetry, this excerpt explores the relationship between humans and nature.

Glossary

rapture — intense happiness
exulting — being very happy
shod — wearing shoes
Confederate — united as a group
chace — another spelling of 'chase'; here it refers to a hunt
precipices — steep sides of a cliff or mountain
tumult — a loud noise, especially one made by a group of people

William Wordsworth

William Wordsworth was a poet from the Lake District. 'The Prelude' is an autobiographical poem —
it explores key moments and experiences in Wordsworth's life. It was published after his death in 1850.

You've got to know what the poem's about

1) The excerpt is written by an adult who is looking back nostalgically on his childhood memories.

2) It begins on a winter evening when the narrator is playing outside. It's getting dark,
which is the time he's supposed to go home, but he doesn't because he's having a good
time. The narrator describes the fun he and his friends are having ice skating.

3) The adult narrator then reflects on nature and suggests that humans are distanced from it.

Learn about the form, structure and language

1) **FORM** — This excerpt is a first-person narrative. As the adult narrator is looking back on his
own memories, it's personal, and his childhood seems almost idyllic. The use of blank verse
and enjambment create a regular rhythm, which makes the poem sound like natural speech.

2) **STRUCTURE** — There are two main sections in the excerpt. The first focuses on the fun the children
are having and the tone is light and carefree. There's a distinct change when the focus of the poem
turns to nature — the tone is more serious as the narrator shows a greater awareness of nature.

3) **LANGUAGE OF MOVEMENT** — The speaker uses short, monosyllabic verbs such as "<u>flew</u>" to
increase the poem's pace. This reflects the speed of their movements and their youthful energy.

4) **ANIMAL IMAGERY** — The narrator compares himself to a horse and the group of children to a
"<u>Pack</u>" of hunting dogs. This could suggest that they have a close connection to nature. However,
dogs and horses are often domesticated, which hints that the children aren't truly a part of nature.

5) **USE OF SOUNDS** — Sibilance and onomatopoeia allow the reader to imagine the
sounds in the poem. The poet also uses sensory imagery to contrast humans and nature
— the humans are noisy, but nature's sounds are more delicate and unusual.

Remember the feelings and attitudes in the poem

1) **NOSTALGIA** — The narrator fondly looks back on his childhood
and presents an idyllic scene from his memories. He uses language
like "<u>exulting</u>" to convey a sense of excitement and freedom.

2) **AWARENESS** — The poem ends with the narrator showing a greater appreciation
of the natural world. The references to the "<u>distant hills</u>" and to the east and
west suggest that he has become more aware of the vast scale of nature.

"Umm... this smile is
hurting now. Can I stop
appreciating nature yet?"

Go a step further and give a personal response

Have a go at answering these questions to help you come up with your own ideas about the poem:

Q1. What is the effect of the repetition of "while" in lines 18 and 20?

Q2. How does the narrator convey that he is in awe of nature?

Q3. What impression of nature do you have by the end of the poem?

Nature, change and transformation, sense of place...

You could contrast the sense of place and awe of nature in this poem with the building in 'Living Space'.
Seamus Heaney's 'Death of a Naturalist' also discusses nature in connection with childhood memories.

Practice Questions

What's that you say? More poetry? Fear not, intrepid English student, for here are some handy questions which cover all the poems you've just read, helping you to check you're getting to grips with each one.

For even more practice, try the Sudden Fail Quiz — just scan this QR code!

Sudden Fail Quiz

The Manhunt

1) How does the poet convey the fragility of the soldier?

2) What is the effect of the repetition in stanzas 4-6?

Sonnet 43

1) Give a summary of what the narrator says in the poem.

2) How does Barrett Browning use hyperbole in the poem?

London

1) How does the poem convey a sense of hopelessness?

2) What do you think might have been Blake's motivation for writing the poem? Think about the context of the poem.

The Soldier

1) How does the narrator emphasise his fondness for the English countryside?

2) Why do you think the narrator directly addresses the reader in the first line?

She Walks in Beauty

1) What do you think the poem's overall message is?

2) Find and explain an example of a time when sound devices contribute to the poem's meaning.

Living Space

Why yes, I am good at impressions.

1) Describe the speaker's attitude towards the building.

2) How does the form of the poem influence the reader's impression of the building?

Practice Questions

As Imperceptibly as Grief

1) Briefly explain what the poem is about.

2) What is unusual about the punctuation in the poem? Explain what effect this punctuation has.

Cozy Apologia

1) Describe the narrator's tone in the poem. What effect does it have?

2) Why do you think the poet includes domestic images in the poem?

Valentine

1) Give a short explanation of the extended metaphor that is used in the poem.

2) How does the mood change throughout the poem?

A Wife in London

1) Briefly describe what happens in the poem.

2) How does the poet create a sense that the tragedy in the poem is unavoidable?

Death of a Naturalist

1) How do the narrator's emotions change over the course of the poem?

2) What techniques are used in the first stanza to convey the narrator's glee?

Hawk Roosting

1) How does the poet present the hawk as being in control?

2) What is the effect of end-stopping in the poem?

Practice Questions

To Autumn

1) How does Keats present nature as constantly changing?

2) What is the effect of the way each stanza of the poem is structured?

Afternoons

1) How does the poem convey a sense of monotony?

2) Why do you think the poem is set as the seasons are changing? What is the effect of this?

Dulce et Decorum Est

1) How does the poet convey strong feelings about war in the poem?

2) What is the effect of Owen's use of realistic images of war?

Ozymandias

1) Who was Ozymandias? Briefly describe his character.

2) How is the power of nature presented in the poem?

King of wings

Mametz Wood

1) What does the speaker's tone reveal about their attitude to the soldiers?

2) Find an example of alliteration in the poem and explain why it has been used.

Excerpt from 'The Prelude'

1) What do you think the overall message of the excerpt is?

2) Describe two different effects created by caesurae in the excerpt.

Practice Questions

Here's a page of exam-style questions for you now. You don't have to do these all at once — just do them in a way that suits you. Before you start, here are some important things you need to remember:

In each of your answers, you should write about how poets use language, structure and form and the effects these create for the reader. It's also important to include some ideas about context — think about how the poets might have been influenced by things like history, culture and their own experiences.

Exam-style Questions

1. i) Owen examines the reality of war in 'Dulce et Decorum Est'.
        Discuss how Owen explores the reality of war through the poem.

    ii) From the anthology, select another poem which examines the reality of war. Compare how this theme is explored in 'Dulce et Decorum Est' and the way it is explored in your selected poem.

2. i) Negative emotions are important in the poem 'Valentine'.
        Examine how Duffy looks at negative emotions through the poem.

    ii) Pick another poem from the anthology which explores negative emotions. Compare how this theme is presented in 'Valentine' and the way it is presented in the poem you have picked.

3. i) Hughes presents the speaker in 'Hawk Roosting' as brutal.
        Explain how Hughes presents the hawk as brutal in the poem.

    ii) Select another poem from the anthology which features brutality. Compare how brutality is conveyed in 'Hawk Roosting' and the way it is conveyed in the poem you have chosen.

4. i) Hardy examines an individual's pain in 'A Wife in London'.
        Discuss how Hardy explores pain through the poem.

    ii) From the anthology, select another poem which examines the theme of pain. Compare how pain is explored in 'A Wife in London' and the way it is explored in the poem you have selected.

5. i) Armitage creates a sense of fragility in 'The Manhunt'.
        Explain how Armitage presents fragility through the poem.

    ii) Select another poem from the anthology which includes ideas about fragility. Compare the way that 'The Manhunt' examines fragility with the way it is examined in your selected poem.

6. i) The theme of change is important in the poem 'Death of a Naturalist'.
        Examine how Heaney looks at change through the poem.

    ii) Pick another poem from the anthology which explores change. Compare how this theme is explored in 'Death of a Naturalist' and the way it is explored in the poem you have picked.

Love and Relationships

The exam will ask you how the poets explore a certain theme, so here are some themes that could come up.

> 1) Love is a **complex concept** which can involve many different feelings.
> 2) Ordinary relationships may have **imperfections**, but they're more **real** than idealised love.

Love can be made up of lots of different emotions

Sonnet 43 (Pages 4-5)

1) The speaker's **hyperbolic expressions** about the "<u>depth and breadth and height</u>" of her love create a sense of **vastness** to contrast with the **intimate** nature of "<u>every day's / Most quiet need</u>". The idea that her love is on both a **large** and a **small scale** suggests she loves the addressee in **different ways**.

2) The speaker mixes **positive** and **negative** emotions when describing the "<u>Smiles, tears</u>" that she has experienced during the course of her life. These emotions **contribute** to her love, and the speaker conveys the idea that these **feelings** and **experiences** are what make her devotion so **strong**.

Valentine (Pages 18-19)

1) The **metaphor** of the onion shows that love involves many **different emotions**, as it "<u>promises light</u>", but also "<u>will blind you with tears</u>". Onions also have many **layers**, which implies that love is made up of **various elements** too.

2) A sense of **ambiguity** is created through the use of both **positive** and **negative language**. The onion's "<u>fierce kiss</u>" is described as "<u>possessive and faithful</u>" — although these adjectives are both describing the same thing, they have very **different connotations** for the reader.

Some poems look at the ordinariness of relationships

Cozy Apologia (Pages 16-17)

1) The speaker is **pleased** with the fact that her current relationship is **ordinary**. She recognises that they're "<u>content, but fall short of the Divine</u>" — she suggests that their love is more **true** because it's **normal** and **realistic**.

2) She uses **humour** to compare the boys she dated with "<u>licorice</u>" and **pokes fun** at their **inexperience** — she recalls how they would "<u>kiss you senseless</u>". It shows that the speaker doesn't idealise **young love** either.

"I could pick anything and think of you — like this chair..."

Afternoons (Pages 28-29)

1) Throughout the poem, the speaker hints that the **relationships** of the women have **changed** over time. They're only referred to as "<u>Young mothers</u>", while the phrases "<u>Behind them</u>" and "<u>Before them</u>" emphasise that the women **aren't** the "<u>lovers</u>" that they were. This suggests that the two identities aren't **compatible** — their only focus is now being "<u>mothers</u>" to their children.

2) The speaker uses domestic images to show how **relationships** are **unappreciated**. A person's wedding day is often considered one of the **best** days of their life, but the fact that the **memories** of this day are "<u>lying</u>" by something as **ordinary** as "<u>the television</u>" implies that the women's **priorities** have **changed**.

Other poems feature the theme of love and relationships...

'She Walks in Beauty' is about the intense, overwhelming attraction the narrator feels for a woman. In 'The Manhunt' and 'A Wife in London', the speakers explore how relationships are affected by war.

Faith and Worship

These themes might seem a little tricky at first, but you can do it — just have a little faith in yourself...

1) **Religious faith** can be used to explore **other emotions**.
2) Worship isn't restricted to **religion** — sometimes a **place** or a **person** is worshipped.

Faith is often connected to other feelings

Sonnet 43 (Pages 4-5)

1) The speaker refers to her "childhood's faith" to show that faith is important in her life. She draws parallels between her feelings of love for the addressee and her soul searching for "ideal Grace".

2) It's as if the speaker finds that religious faith comes so naturally to her that it impacts on how she thinks about other aspects of her life, including the definition of love.

3) The link made between religious faith and romantic love makes them seem similar — this is reinforced by the idea that she will love him "better after death" and her hope that God will support their love.

Living Space (Pages 12-13)

1) The speaker uses the nature of the building and the placement of the eggs to convey ideas about faith.

2) Religious language is used to establish a connection between the building and faith. The fact that the building "leans dangerously / towards the miraculous" hints that belief in the building's structure involves the same sort of faith that it takes to believe in miracles.

3) Placing the eggs in a dangerous place requires trust and faith that they'll be alright. The fact that the eggshells are described as the "bright, thin walls of faith" suggests that even when people have faith, it can waver. Dharker might be implying that having religious faith can be difficult.

Sometimes people worship a place or an individual

The Soldier (Pages 8-9)

1) By choosing to write the poem in the form of a sonnet, which is usually used for love poetry, Brooke emphasises how much the speaker worships England. The repetition of "England" in the poem makes it sound as if his country is the most important thing to him — it dominates his thoughts.

2) England is personified both as a mother figure and as a godlike one. The speaker worships its abilities and beauty — it "bore" him, gave him life and created a heavenly paradise full of "flowers" and "rivers". The fact that the speaker has been "blest" makes England seem even more like a god.

She Walks in Beauty (Pages 10-11)

1) The use of hyperbole in "all that's best of dark and bright" shows that the woman described is perfect. The speaker focuses on different parts of the woman's body, such as her "raven tress" and her "cheek" — each one is worthy of being worshipped.

2) The speaker suggests that the woman is divine. He describes the way that her mind is "at peace with all below", which could imply she's above everyone else, possibly like an angel or goddess.

Other poems also look at worship...

In 'To Autumn', the speaker worships autumn and shows great appreciation for all that it produces for humans, such as fruit. In 'Hawk Roosting', the hawk is a very proud creature that almost worships itself.

Passage of Time

Whoa, doesn't time just fly when you're having fun and studying poems about the passage of time?

1) The passage of time **isn't** always a **good thing** — it can have a **negative impact** on people.

2) Time sometimes moves in **cycles**, instead of in a linear way.

Time passing can have a negative effect

Afternoons (Pages 28-29)

1) The poem is set as "<u>Summer is fading</u>", which reflects the transitional moment the women are at in their lives. Summer represents their finest days, while the arrival of autumn has negative connotations for their future. It suggests the women's lives are "<u>fading</u>" — they're losing their vibrancy.

2) The speaker makes the observation that the women's "<u>beauty has thickened</u>". The word "<u>thickened</u>" suggests their looks have deteriorated, revealing that time has passed. This implies that youth is short-lived — the speaker's slightly cruel tone may be reflecting the harsh nature of time.

Ozymandias (Pages 32-33)

1) Ozymandias is increasingly **forgotten about** as time passes. His statue has **disintegrated** over time, leaving a "<u>shattered visage</u>" and "<u>trunkless legs</u>". This emphasises that Ozymandias's rule was only **temporary**, and hints that his legacy will eventually be **lost** completely.

2) The **setting** of the poem is only described as "<u>an antique land</u>", and there's **no information** about the **speaker** or the "<u>traveller</u>" they talk to, which gives the poem a sense of **timelessness**. It suggests that the **passage of time**, and the **decay** this causes, is happening **constantly**.

Time often has a cyclical nature

As Imperceptibly as Grief (Pages 14-15)

1) The **personified** summer's "<u>light escape</u>" is a **metaphor** for the **disappearance** of the speaker's **grief** over time. The **seasons** only last for a certain time before they **change**, which could suggest that the amount of time a person can spend grieving is also **limited**.

2) Different **images of light** (such as "<u>Twilight</u>", "<u>Dusk</u>" and the "<u>foreign</u>" light of morning) remind the reader that **day** and **night** are part of a **natural cycle**. These images reflect aspects of the speaker's **grieving process** — she might be suggesting that **life** and **death** are part of a natural cycle too.

To Autumn (Pages 26-27)

1) Autumn is **praised** for filling "<u>all fruit with ripeness to the core</u>" in the first stanza by the speaker, who later describes how "<u>the light wind lives or dies</u>". The images of **life and death** show that time moves in a **circular** way.

2) An image of "<u>gathering swallows</u>" shows that time's cyclical nature provides a reason to be **hopeful**. Swallows move with the **seasons** — despite their **departure** in the winter, they will **return** in the spring.

"It could've been worse — they could've dressed me up like a pumpkin too..."

Other poems also look at the passage of time...

In 'Death of a Naturalist', Heaney uses the passage of time to show how people's attitudes can change. The speaker in 'Mametz Wood' shows how time passing can help to heal the damage caused by war.

Change and Transformation

If you want change, I've got plenty over here — the vending machine gave me back loads of it.

1) Change is **unpredictable** and **uncontrollable** — it just happens.
2) **People** don't stay the **same** — their **opinions** often change over time.

Change often happens unexpectedly

As Imperceptibly as Grief (Pages 14-15)

1) Summer's disappearance is described as "imperceptible" — the speaker **hardly realises** it has gone. The word "imperceptible" echoes "imperceptibly" from the first line, making it seem as though the poem only **progresses gradually** and reinforcing the idea that change can be **subtle**.

2) Summer's **escape** in the final stanza represents the **end** of the speaker's grieving process. Summer is **temporary** in nature, which implies that grief will **fade away**, even if the speaker doesn't want it to. This suggests that **change** is often **uncontrollable**.

Afternoons (Pages 28-29)

1) The women in the poem are experiencing changes that are **uncontrollable**. The narrator describes how "the wind / Is ruining their courting places", suggesting that nature is behind the changes in their lives. **Leaves** are also used to represent change — they fall in "ones and twos", reinforcing the idea that change **isn't predictable** and **happens gradually**.

2) The narrator states that "Something" is forcing the women "To the side of their own lives", implying that it's **difficult** to identify the **source** of change, even when it has a **profound effect** on people.

People's views can transform as they grow up

Death of a Naturalist (Pages 22-23)

1) Dividing the poem into **two stanzas** emphasises the **contrasting views** the speaker holds over time. Words used in the first stanza which link to **decay**, such as "festered", hint at the **change** in attitude to come and **foreshadow** the way the narrator loses his **childhood enthusiasm**.

2) The poem's **title** also emphasises the **change** in viewpoint. The word "Death" is an extreme description of how the child **loses** his love of nature. It also suggests that he's lost his **innocence** as he's grown up — he's seen a **dark side** to nature that he didn't see as a child.

Excerpt from 'The Prelude' (Pages 36-37)

1) As a **child**, the narrator was more interested in playing with his **friends** than in appreciating nature. Towards the end of the excerpt, there is a **change in focus**, and the adult narrator considers **nature** more closely. This suggests that growing up involves becoming more **conscious** of what's around you.

2) The narrator **doesn't criticise** his younger self for his lack of awareness. He reflects on how nature's sounds were "not unnoticed" by him as a child — the **double negative** here could hint that the natural world is **difficult** to fully understand and appreciate.

Change and transformation feature in other poems...

In 'Ozymandias', change over time is evident from the ruined statue and words of the king himself. 'To Autumn' charts the way autumn turns into winter — Keats uses imagery to show change happening.

Pain and Suffering

This page is all about the themes of pain and suffering. Could be worse — you could be doing Maths...

1) Suffering can be specific to an individual, or it can affect many people.
2) Some events, such as war, are so traumatic that they cause physical and emotional pain.

Suffering can be a collective or individual experience

London (Pages 6-7)

1) The speaker sees lots of people suffering on the streets of London. The repetition of the words "cry" and "every" emphasises the extent of the suffering, while the reference to "plagues" suggests physical pain and suffering caused by illness.

2) There's also an absence of hope, with no sense that anyone can do anything to improve the situation. The final image of the plagued "Marriage hearse" implies the cycle of suffering will continue.

A Wife in London (Pages 20-21)

1) The wife's emotional suffering is foreshadowed by images of light being overcome by darkness — "The street-lamp glimmers cold" like a "waning taper". This suggests any warmth in her life is gone.

2) Weather imagery shows that her suffering has worsened the day after she hears about her husband's death — the "fog hangs thicker", just as her pain and distress have intensified.

3) By vaguely referring to "A Wife" in the title, Hardy could be suggesting that the suffering she experiences was common during the war and that many other women experienced similar pain.

People can suffer physically and emotionally

Dulce et Decorum Est (Pages 30-31)

1) The speaker graphically describes the suffering experienced by a fellow soldier. Images such as "froth-corrupted lungs" and "white eyes writhing" vividly present his excruciating pain.

2) Witnessing the soldier's death causes the speaker emotional suffering — he explains that the images of the soldier dying continue to haunt him afterwards.

3) The poem undermines the "old Lie" that dying in war is honourable by raising awareness about the horrors of war. The speaker believes that people would change their minds if they knew the truth, which could save many other young men from suffering a similar fate.

The Manhunt (Pages 2-3)

1) The ex-soldier suffers both physically and emotionally after going to war. His physical injuries, such as "the blown hinge of his lower jaw" and "the fractured rudder of shoulder-blade" are described first, as they're the most obvious.

2) As his wife tries to understand what he's going through, she realises the root of his suffering is "buried deep in his mind". His emotional scarring is difficult to reach and is described as an "unexploded mine", suggesting it continues to affect him and makes him unstable.

Pain and suffering come up in other poems...

The speaker in 'Mametz Wood' personifies the land and shows it has been wounded by World War One. In 'As Imperceptibly as Grief', the speaker suffers emotionally when she realises she's stopped grieving.

Death and Loss

Carrying on with the not-so-cheery themes — here are some poems which look at death and loss.

> 1) **Death** can be portrayed in **different ways** — some see it **positively**, but others **suffer** greatly.
>
> 2) **Loss** is a **complicated emotion** and many people **struggle** with it.

Death and loss can cause pain...

A Wife in London (Pages 20-21)

1) **Loss** is presented as something **unavoidable** in war through the title of the first part, "**I – The Tragedy**". In **classical tragedies**, the main character's suffering is often presented as **inevitable**, so the reader of the poem might **anticipate** the worst right from the start.

2) The poet uses **dashes** to emphasise the wife's **struggle** to comprehend her loss and begin grieving. It suggests that even if a person **knows** that they may lose a loved one, it's still **difficult** to deal with.

Mametz Wood (Pages 34-35)

1) The speaker implies that the soldiers in the poem died a **painful death** as their bodies are "**a broken mosaic of bone**". Their deaths haven't been recognised properly — their body parts are **scattered** across fields and their efforts in the war go **unremembered**.

2) The poem shows how war causes **lasting pain** on a **large scale**. The land is "**working a foreign body to the surface**", showing that recovery is an **ongoing** process.

3) Discovering the soldiers' bodies is an opportunity to **remember** their **pain** and **sacrifice**.

...or they can be comforting

The Soldier (Pages 8-9)

1) The speaker presents death as **peaceful** and **idyllic**, which **contrasts** with the painful deaths of many soldiers during World War One. He associates death with being able to **give** something **back** to **England**, since it's given him so much.

2) Death is a way for the soldier to become closer to **God**, the "**eternal mind**", and could also provide a **release** from the pain he's experiencing at war. The poem could be the soldier's way of making death seem less **daunting**, as he believes it will lead to something **better** than he has now.

As Imperceptibly as Grief (Pages 14-15)

1) Initially, the speaker struggles to accept the end of both **summer** and **grief**. She suggests it's not "**Perfidy**" (betrayal), but she still feels a **sense of loss**. The **personification** of "**Morning**" as a "**Guest**" further develops this — she found the guest (which may symbolise summer or grief) comforting.

2) In the final lines of the poem, however, the **lack** of **dashes** creates a less hesitant tone, suggesting the speaker is more **sure** of herself and has **come to terms** with the fact that she has finished grieving.

3) The poem therefore shows that feelings of loss aren't entirely **negative** and can provide **comfort**, but also that the end of grief is a **positive** change, even if it involves **losing** that sense of comfort.

Other poems also cover death and loss...

In 'Dulce et Decorum Est', the speaker witnesses the death of a soldier and struggles to deal with it. 'To Autumn' discusses the death and decay that comes with the end of autumn and the start of winter.

Effects of War

The effects of war can be pretty painful — I should know, I grew up with two brothers...

1) War causes widespread suffering and has a profound impact on those affected.

2) Many individuals are affected by war, including the families of those who've died.

The effects of war can be seen through groups of soldiers...

Dulce et Decorum Est (Pages 30-31)

1) The speaker is part of a group of soldiers who've been affected physically by the war. He describes how they are "Bent double" and "Knock-kneed" as a result of what they've been through.

2) Using the plural "we" in the first stanza shows they've experienced war collectively, which is emphasised through the idea that they "all" suffer that same problems. This contrasts with the direct address to "you" in the final stanza, making the speaker's tone seem more confrontational.

Mametz Wood (Pages 34-35)

1) The speaker shows that the soldiers suffered physically — he describes broken body parts individually to emphasise the dehumanising nature of war. Images of "socketed heads" and "the china plate of a shoulder blade" show how the men have lost their identities.

2) An effect of war shown in the poem is soldiers being forgotten about. The speaker seeks to show the importance of remembrance and give these soldiers a voice, even if their "tongues" are "absent".

...and through the effect on the individual

The Manhunt (Pages 2-3)

1) The speaker shows that the effects of war can last long after the fighting has ended. She picks out specific injuries the ex-soldier has sustained (like "broken ribs") as well as the "unexploded mine" that represents the psychological injuries he still suffers from.

2) War has also affected his relationship with his wife. She is trying to understand his suffering, but he is still in so much pain from the trauma that her progress is limited — she can only "come close" to 'finding' him again. The title 'The Manhunt' shows that an effect of war is soldiers finding themselves 'lost' to those who know them best — conflict makes them unrecognisable.

A Wife in London (Pages 20-21)

1) The poem looks at how individuals are affected by the death of a loved one at war. The dashes in the second stanza show the wife's distress after learning that her husband has died. Furthermore, the reference to "new love" in the final stanza could imply that any children they'd planned to have won't be born — the rest of the woman's life has changed beyond recognition.

2) In the final stanza, the speaker suggests that war is a waste — it has cut short the life of a promising young man. Descriptions of the husband's writing as "Fresh" and "firm" suggest he had so much more to offer, but ironically it was these qualities that meant that he was fit for war in the first place.

OTHER POEMS

The effects of war are shown in 'The Soldier'...

'The Soldier' doesn't mention the horrifying aspects of war — the speaker looks at death positively and believes it will allow him to give something back. He finds it comforting to think about his homeland.

Negative Emotions

You might have some negative emotions towards poetry by now, but at least this page has some cute animals.

1) **Pride** is linked to **power**, and it often leads to a **misuse** of that power.

2) **Anger** can stem from a sense of **mistreatment** or from **frustration** at others' attitudes.

Too much pride can lead to arrogance

Hawk Roosting (Pages 24-25)

1) The hawk is very **arrogant** and sees itself as the most **powerful** creature in nature. It says "**I hold Creation in my foot**", implying that it even preys upon **God**. The hawk doesn't even consider the possibility of its **power** being **challenged**, which makes it seem particularly arrogant. Some people might think this makes the hawk seem **naive** — death and loss of power are **inevitable** parts of life.

2) Arrogance makes the hawk **abusive** — it explains "**I kill where I please because it is all mine**".

Ozymandias (Pages 32-33)

1) The words on the pedestal of the statue show that Ozymandias was a **proud**, **arrogant ruler**. He calls himself the "**king of kings**" and commands others to "**Look**" at his works and "**despair**".

2) Ozymandias's "**sneer of cold command**" suggests that he thought everyone else was **inferior** to him, and that he treated his subjects **badly**. The fact that the sculptor **incorporated** his sneer into the **statue** shows that it was a **defining part** of his character. This creates a sense of **irony** — even though Ozymandias's **power** has gone, evidence of his **pride** remains.

Anger can be directed at society

London (Pages 6-7)

1) The narrator is angry about the **society** he sees as he **wanders** the streets of London.

2) He uses **rhetorical devices** to get the reader to share his anger. For example, he **repeats** "**marks**" and "**every**" and uses **emotive imagery**, such as "**every Infant's cry of fear**".

3) Powerful images of the "**black'ning Church**" and the "**blood down Palace walls**" show his anger at institutions like the **Church** and **political leaders** for not **improving** things.

"I'm so angry that everyone gets us mixed up... we don't look anything like each other!"

Dulce et Decorum Est (Pages 30-31)

1) The narrator **criticises** the idea that dying in war is **honourable**. He juxtaposes **graphic images** of a dying soldier with the 'noble' **Latin phrase** that expresses this idea to expose its **inaccuracy**.

2) By addressing the reader as "**My friend**", the speaker stresses the difference of opinion between them. He refers to the Latin phrase as the "**old Lie**", emphasising his **dislike** of it. The final line, "**Pro patria mori**", is dramatically **shorter** than the rest — this could be the speaker's way of suggesting that this **belief** is the reason why the lives of so many young men are **cut short**.

Other poems also feature negative emotions...

The second stanza of 'Death of a Naturalist' is very negative as the speaker experiences feelings of disgust. 'Valentine' includes dangerous language, which reveals the speaker's mixed emotions about love.

Nature

The sky outside is a dull, dreary grey. Not a reflection of my mood, just what the weather's like. Again.

1) Nature is sometimes **praised** for the incredible things it can do.
2) There's a side to nature which can be **violent** and **fearsome**.

Some poems praise nature...

To Autumn (Pages 26-27)

1) Keats wrote the poem as an ode, a form of poetry typically written to praise something, highlighting his high regard for autumn.

2) The speaker focuses on the richness of autumn and what the season provides. Detailed images like the "moss'd cottage-trees" and verbs such as "swell" and "o'erbrimm'd" convey the speaker's joy at the abundance of the season.

3) At the start of the third stanza, the speaker reassures autumn that it has its own music, as if defending it from those who don't share his love of it. His negativity towards spring further shows how important autumn is to him.

Excerpt from 'The Prelude' (Pages 36-37)

1) The excerpt has a distinct volta where the focus shifts to nature. Whereas the narrator's childhood self was more interested in playing, his adult self muses on the awe-inspiring qualities of nature.

2) The sounds of nature are different to the familiar sounds of the people — "Tinkled" and "alien" show how the speaker admires nature because it's so different to humanity.

...while others examine its threatening side

Death of a Naturalist (Pages 22-23)

1) The narrator fears nature in the second stanza — his descriptions suggest that nature has a dark side. Language associated with the military, such as the simile comparing the frogs to "mud grenades", implies that he feels threatened by them.

2) The poem ends with the disconcerting image of the speaker's hand being clutched by the frogspawn in an act of "vengeance". It's ironic that nature gains more power over the narrator as he ages, not the other way around as the reader might expect.

Hawk Roosting (Pages 24-25)

1) The hawk is violent and practises "**perfect kills**" in its sleep, while its cruel nature means that its "**manners are tearing off heads**". Its matter-of-fact tone regarding violence is shocking for the reader. As a bird, the hawk is part of nature, so its violence suggests that brutality is a part of nature itself.

2) By showing the brutality of the food chain through the hawk, the poem could be implying that nature has a self-destructive side. Perhaps Hughes was challenging the reader's expectation that poetry about nature always focuses on its pleasant aspects.

OTHER POEMS

Nature is an important theme in other poems...

The narrator of 'Mametz Wood' personifies the earth and shows that nature is preserving the memory of the soldiers. In 'The Soldier', the speaker presents the English countryside as idyllic and peaceful.

Sense of Place

I always find that falling asleep on the bus makes me lose my sense of place... and miss my stop.

> 1) **Urban places** can inspire **hope** or leave people feeling **hopeless**.
>
> 2) Some present **natural settings** as **homely** and **familiar**, while others view them as **awe-inspiring**.

Sense of place could mean an urban setting...

London (Pages 6-7)

1) The speaker **doesn't engage** with the setting — he just **observes** and **comments** on the **bigger picture**, making his words seem more **convincing**. His description of the city of London is entirely **negative**. Images of suffering such as <u>"the new born Infant's tear"</u> suggest that the **setting** confines people to a life of **despair**, while <u>"blights with plagues"</u> suggests **death** and **destruction**.

2) By describing the Thames as <u>"charter'd"</u>, the narrator suggests that even the river has had its freedom **limited** by society. This hints that the city's **problems** are deeply **entrenched** and will be **hard to solve**.

Living Space (Pages 12-13)

1) The first stanza includes **enjambment** and **caesurae** which create a sense of **jerkiness** and **disorder**. The chaotic nature of the poem reflects the **haphazard** nature of the **building** Dharker describes.

2) The building in the poem is described as being part of a <u>"slanted universe"</u>. This suggests that it is supposed to be a small-scale **representation** of a larger place. Here, the <u>"universe"</u> might refer either to **Mumbai**, the city Dharker was inspired by, or to the **whole world**.

...or the natural environment

The Soldier (Pages 8-9)

1) The speaker reminisces about the **beauty** of the **English countryside**. The positive imagery of the <u>"flowers"</u>, <u>"rivers"</u> and <u>"suns"</u> creates a **picturesque** scene. The images of England in the soldier's imagination **contrast** with his **actual location** — a <u>"foreign field"</u> where he is fighting in a **war**.

2) By not focusing on where the speaker is, Brooke emphasises the **importance** of **England**. In **death**, the speaker seeks to make the land where he is buried <u>"for ever England"</u>. This shows that his **attachment** to his country is so **strong** that it can almost **transform** the place he's in.

Excerpt from 'The Prelude' (Pages 36-37)

1) The speaker describes the scene of <u>"leafless trees"</u> and <u>"distant hills"</u> around him. The <u>"din"</u> from the humans contrasts with the <u>"alien sound"</u> of nature, establishing a **separation** between the **people** and their **surroundings**.

2) Nature's sounds are <u>"not unnoticed"</u> by the narrator, which suggests that humans can **perceive** nature and be in **awe** of it, but hints that they still **struggle** to **understand** it fully.

3) **Caesurae** in the last few lines make the speaker seem more **reflective** and **perceptive** of his surroundings. This shows that people can have a **changing relationship** with their **environment**.

Think about sense of place in other poems...

'Cozy Apologia' creates a sense of a safe, indoor place where the speaker is sheltering from a hurricane. In 'Afternoons', the poem's setting is familiar and specific, but also could apply to many different places.

Context

These two pages give you some juicy nuggets of context — use them wisely to help you write great answers.

Context helps you to show wider knowledge

1) To get a top grade, you need to explain how the ideas in the poems relate to their context.

2) When you're thinking about a particular poem, consider these aspects of context:

Historical — Do the ideas in the poem relate to the time in which it's written or set?

Geographical — How is the poem shaped and influenced by the place in which it's set?

Social — Is the poet criticising or praising the society or community they're writing about?

Cultural — Does the poet draw on a particular aspect of their background or culture?

Literary — Was the poet influenced by other works of literature or a particular literary movement?

3) These pages explore some contextual aspects of the poems, but you should also do some of your own research about each poem's context.

See page 73 for some tips and tricks on how to include context in your exam answer.

War is often idealised but has a tragic reality

1) During many wars, governments and the media used propaganda to encourage soldiers to fight. They glorified war by presenting soldiers as patriotic heroes and depicted death as a noble sacrifice.

2) This idealistic view was common at the beginning of World War One. The narrator in 'The Soldier' is devoted to his country and willing to die for it — he calmly pictures his grave in a "foreign field".

Dulce et Decorum Est (Pages 30-31)

Owen fought in World War One and wrote about the realities of war:

- The narrator describes a man "drowning" from a gas attack. The vivid, horrific images in the poem contradict the idealistic depictions of war.

- The poem bitterly condemns the "old Lie" that it was an honour to die for your country, using reality to reject patriotic propaganda.

Relevant Poems

The Manhunt
The Soldier
A Wife in London
Dulce et Decorum Est
Mametz Wood

3) Hardy criticised the Boer War as pointless and tragic, and wrote several poems influenced by these views. 'A Wife in London' reflects the hopelessness, enduring heartbreak and waste of life that is caused by war.

4) 'The Manhunt' was inspired by a soldier who suffered from PTSD (post-traumatic stress disorder) as a result of his experiences in war. The narrator's focus on her husband's physical and mental pain firmly rejects glorified ideas of war, instead revealing the traumatic impact that it has on soldiers and their loved ones.

5) In 'Mametz Wood', the discovery of the bodies of the "wasted young" decades after their deaths suggests that their sacrifice has not been appreciated by the society they died for, and emphasises the tragedy of war.

Poetry elevates the ordinary

1) In 'Afternoons', Larkin explores people's lives through an everyday scene at a "recreation ground". Much of Larkin's work focuses on the realities of life in postwar Britain — by capturing this in his poetry, he celebrated the ordinary aspects of life.

Relevant Poems

Cozy Apologia
Valentine
Afternoons

2) 'Cozy Apologia' and 'Valentine' both replace traditional images of love with everyday objects. In 'Cozy Apologia', the narrator associates her partner with a "lamp" and her "pen", while the narrator in Valentine offers their lover "an onion".

3) The use of domestic images celebrates the ordinary aspects of relationships and suggests the love is real.

Context

Faith can shape people's understanding of the world...

1) **Religion** can provide a **reference point** for understanding and processing **experiences**.

2) In 'Sonnet 43', the speaker compares her **romantic love** to her "childhood's faith". Her love gives her life **meaning** in the same way as **religious faith** can.

3) The narrator in 'Living Space' suggests that **faith** keeps the "miraculous" building standing — this **faith** gives people **hope** for the future and helps them **endure difficulties**.

> **Relevant Poems**
>
> Sonnet 43
>
> Living Space

...and so can nature

1) Poets often turn to the **natural world** to attempt to **understand** human **experience**.

2) In 'Cozy Apologia', the **danger** of the approaching **hurricane** makes the narrator think about her partner, who represents **safety** and **comfort**. Hurricane Floyd's **temporary nature** (and its unlikely name) also reminds her of **past relationships**.

3) In 'As Imperceptibly as Grief', the narrator likens the **changing seasons** to the **grieving process**. 'Afternoons' also uses the **seasons** as a **metaphor** to explore different **life stages** — the "fading" summer reflects the mothers' **loss of youth** and **freedom**.

4) 'Death of a Naturalist' uses nature to consider **how people change** as they age. The natural world initially **inspires powerful emotion** and **admiration** in the narrator, but later they're "sickened" by the frogspawn.

> **Relevant Poems**
>
> As Imperceptibly as Grief
>
> Cozy Apologia
>
> Death of a Naturalist
>
> Hawk Roosting
>
> Afternoons

> ### Hawk Roosting (Pages 24-25)
>
> - Some readers have interpreted the poem as an **allegory** for **human nature** (see p.24) — the hawk's **arrogance** could help the reader to understand the **mindset** of violent, **tyrannical** human **leaders**.
> - The poem could also help humans to **appreciate** the **natural world** and their **relationship** with it.

Romanticism was a movement in art and literature

1) Romanticism was a **movement** in the late 18th and early 19th century. The Romantics **reacted** against an increased emphasis on **science** and **rationality** (the 'Enlightenment').

2) The **Romantic poets**, e.g. Percy Bysshe **Shelley**, William **Blake**, John **Keats**, Lord **Byron** and William **Wordsworth**, were at the centre of this movement.

> **Relevant Poems**
>
> She Walks in Beauty   London
>
> Ozymandias   To Autumn
>
> Excerpt from 'The Prelude'

3) Many of these poets **shared** key **ideas**:

- The concept of 'the **sublime**'. This term describes the **feeling of awe** that someone might **experience** when encountering the **power** of **nature** — e.g. in 'To Autumn', Keats's narrator feels a sense of wonder when they exclaim over the "mellow fruitfulness!" of the season.

- **Closeness to nature**. They celebrated **childhood innocence** as a state that brought people closer to nature — e.g. in 'The Prelude', the scene is "a time of rapture", revealing the narrator's **intense joy** in nature as a **child**. The Romantics also stressed the **beauty** of **nature** — e.g. 'She Walks in Beauty' uses natural imagery to **praise** the woman's appearance, showing **admiration** for the **natural world**.

- **Anti-establishment political ideals**. The Romantics believed people should exercise their individual **freedom** rather than follow imposed rules, and **disliked oppression** and **fixed hierarchies** — e.g. in 'Ozymandias', the ruined statue of a king reflects Shelley's ideal that **tyrants** can be **overturned**.

- **Responsibility** to **ordinary people**. They felt poetry should **inform** people and **change society**. E.g. Blake addresses **social issues** in 'London' by highlighting the **suffering** of city-dwellers.

Practice Questions

There are some exam-style questions just around the corner, but first here are some questions that you don't need to write a full essay to answer. One or two short paragraphs should be enough.

For even more practice, try the Sudden Fail Quiz — just scan this QR code!

Sudden Fail Quiz

Love and Relationships

1) How does Barrett Browning use language to show the strength of her love in 'Sonnet 43'?

2) What is the effect of Duffy's use of contrasting language in 'Valentine'?

3) In 'Cozy Apologia', how do you think the speaker's experiences of love have affected her?

Faith and Worship

1) In 'Living Space', how does the speaker use the building to comment on religious faith?

2) How does the speaker in 'The Soldier' make England seem divine?

3) How does the imagery in 'She Walks in Beauty' emphasise the speaker's infatuation?

Passage of Time

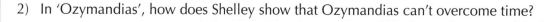

1) How does Larkin suggest that the women in 'Afternoons' are being treated badly by time?

2) In 'Ozymandias', how does Shelley show that Ozymandias can't overcome time?

3) How do the images of nature in 'To Autumn' convey the passing of time?

Change and Transformation

1) In 'As Imperceptibly as Grief', what does the structure of the first three lines imply about change?

2) In 'Afternoons', how does Larkin use nature to show that change is uncontrollable?

3) How do the form and title of 'Death of a Naturalist' highlight the change in the speaker's attitude?

Pain and Suffering

1) How does the narrator of 'London' convey the idea that the suffering in the city is never-ending?

2) In 'Dulce et Decorum Est', how does Owen present physical and emotional suffering?

3) In 'The Manhunt', how does the poet suggest that the soldier's emotional suffering is more difficult to deal with than his physical suffering?

Practice Questions

Death and Loss

1) How is the wife's sense of loss presented in 'A Wife in London'?

2) In 'The Soldier', what does the narrator believe that he will be able to achieve in death?

3) How is the speaker's gradual acceptance of grief shown in 'As Imperceptibly as Grief'?

Effects of War

1) How does Owen use plurals to show how widespread the effects of war are 'Dulce et Decorum Est'?

2) In 'Mametz Wood', how does the poet convey the idea that war can take away soldiers' identities?

3) How does the speaker's language show the impact of war on the woman in 'A Wife in London'?

Negative Emotions

1) How does Hughes present the hawk's cruelty in 'Hawk Roosting'?

2) In 'Ozymandias', how is Ozymandias's pride shown through his statue?

3) Do you think the speaker's anger at society comes across more strongly in 'London' or in 'Dulce et Decorum Est'? Explain your answer.

Nature

1) How does the speaker in 'To Autumn' illustrate that autumn is plentiful?

2) How does Heaney use language to make the frogs seem intimidating in 'Death of a Naturalist'?

3) In 'Hawk Roosting', why do you think Hughes chose a hawk to be the voice of nature?

Sense of Place

1) In 'London', how does the narrator present the city in a negative way?

2) In 'Living Space', how is the fragility of the building demonstrated through language?

3) How does the poet convey the speaker's separation from nature in the excerpt from 'The Prelude'?

Practice Questions

When it comes to the exam, you'll write about a theme in one poem for the first part of the question, then you'll compare two poems in the second part. Tricky stuff, I know, but these questions are good practice.

You'll need to write about the language, structure and form that the poets use for both parts i) and ii), as well as commenting on the effects that these create. You'll have to discuss the context of the poems too — things like how history, culture or the poet's experiences could have had an influence on the poem.

Exam-style Questions

1. i) Religious faith is important in the poem 'Sonnet 43'.
        Examine how Barrett Browning looks at religious faith through the poem.

    ii) Pick another poem from the anthology which explores religious faith. Compare how this theme is explored in 'Sonnet 43' and the way it is explored in the poem you have picked.

2. i) Larkin presents time passing as having a negative effect in 'Afternoons'.
        Explain how Larkin presents the passage of time negatively in the poem.

    ii) Select another poem from the anthology which features time passing. Compare how time passing is conveyed in 'Afternoons' and the way it is conveyed in the poem you have chosen.

3. i) Sheers explores the theme of suffering in 'Mametz Wood'.
        Examine how Sheers presents suffering through the poem.

    ii) From the anthology, select another poem which explores suffering. Compare how this theme is examined in 'Mametz Wood' and the way it is examined in your selected poem.

4. i) Dove presents the speaker's relationship as ordinary in 'Cozy Apologia'.
        Discuss how Dove presents an ordinary relationship in the poem.

    ii) From the anthology, pick another poem which examines relationships. Compare how relationships are explored in 'Cozy Apologia' and the way they are explored in your selected poem.

5. i) The theme of death is important in the poem 'The Soldier'.
        Examine how Brooke looks at death through the poem.

    ii) Pick another poem from the anthology which explores the theme of death. Compare how this theme is conveyed in 'The Soldier' and the way it is conveyed in the poem you have chosen.

6. i) The speaker in the excerpt from 'The Prelude' seems to enjoy being surrounded by nature.
        Explain how Wordsworth presents nature positively through the poem.

    ii) Select another poem from the anthology which features nature. Compare the way that the excerpt from 'The Prelude' examines nature and the way it is examined in your selected poem.

Forms of Poetry

Form is about the rules poets follow when writing poetry. And like all good rules, they're there to be broken...

1) Form can be **rigid** and **regular** or **loose** and **irregular**.

2) Poets **choose** a form to create different **moods** and **effects**.

Hearing poems read aloud can help you identify their features. You can listen to a recording of each poem by using the code at the front of the book.

Some poems have a strict, regular form...

Sonnet 43 (Pages 4-5)

1) Barrett Browning's poem follows a strict **Petrarchan sonnet form** and is written in consistent **iambic pentameter**. This could imply that the narrator's feelings for her lover are **pure**.

2) Petrarchan sonnets **often** present a **problem** in the octave (the first eight lines), and then a **solution** in the sestet (the remaining six lines). 'Sonnet 43' **doesn't** do this, which suggests the speaker believes their love is **perfect** as it is — this reinforces the idea at the end of the poem that her love is **divine**.

She Walks in Beauty (Pages 10-11)

1) The poem has a **rigid form** — it has three six-line stanzas with lines of similar length, and a **consistent** ABABAB rhyme scheme. The **regularity** of this form reflects the woman's **enduring beauty**.

2) The ABABAB rhyme scheme also emphasises how the woman's beauty is made up of a contrast between dark and light. These features **balance** each other out to produce her **perfect beauty**.

...whereas others have a less rigid form

Living Space (Pages 12-13)

1) Dharker's poem is **irregular** — its lines and stanzas vary in length — and it is written in **free verse** to reflect the **irregularity** of the building described. Occasional **rhymes**, such as "<u>Beams</u>" and "<u>seams</u>", could reflect how the building is **loosely held together** by nails.

2) The extensive use of **enjambment** reflects how **ramshackle** the building is, but also suggests it might **spill out** onto other buildings — it's part of a **jumble** of similarly uneven, unstable houses.

3) Long lines appear next to very short ones, which emphasises how the structure is "<u>dangerously</u>" close to **falling down**. It also provides a visual representation of the idea that the whole universe is "<u>slanted</u>".

Valentine (Pages 18-19)

1) 'Valentine' is written in **free verse**, which gives the poem a **conversational** tone, as if the narrator is **directly speaking** to her lover, as well as to the reader.

2) It has short lines, and three of the poem's seven stanzas are only one line long. This irregularity suggests a **break away** from the **conventions** of more traditional love poetry and mirrors the way that the narrator **rejects** commonplace symbols of love, preferring to demonstrate love in **her own way**.

3) The poem has a very **broken-up form**. Each stanza could symbolise a **layer** of the onion which gets **peeled away** as the couple get closer and closer to **understanding** the complex **meaning of love**.

Many poems use specific forms...

'Ozymandias' is also a sonnet, but it doesn't use a traditional sonnet rhyme scheme. 'Hawk Roosting' is a dramatic monologue, where a single speaker (the hawk) addresses an implied audience (mankind).

Poetic Devices

Poets use devices to jazz up their writing. Here are some of the important ones, but there are lots more.

> 1) You need to be able to identify different techniques used in the poems and compare them.
>
> 2) It's important that you don't just say what the technique is — comment on its effect too.

Punctuation affects how a poem flows

Hawk Roosting (Pages 24-25)

1) When the hawk claims that the path of its flight is "direct / Through the bones of the living", the enjambment emphasises the ease with which it can take life.

2) End-stopping makes the hawk sound sure of itself, creating a sense of control in the poem.

Mametz Wood (Pages 34-35)

1) The caesurae in lines 4-5 ("A chit of bone, the china plate of a shoulder blade, / the relic of a finger,") create pauses to focus the reader's attention on each body part.

2) The way the caesurae split the lines up also reflects how the bones are scattered across the wood.

Repetition can be used to reinforce a point

Sonnet 43 (Pages 4-5)

1) Repetition of "I love thee" at the beginnings of lines (anaphora) emphasises the speaker's love.

2) The narrator loves the addressee to the "depth and breadth and height" her "soul can reach", which is an example of hyperbole that uses repetition of "and" to suggest her love is unlimited.

She Walks in Beauty (Pages 10-11)

1) Repetition of "so" in "So soft, so calm" emphasises how much the narrator is astounded by the woman's beauty — he is appreciative of it almost to the point where he sounds obsessive.

2) Additionally, repeating "one" in "One shade the more, one ray the less" reinforces the antithesis in the line — the contrast between the "shade" and "ray" is balanced perfectly to match her beauty.

Sounds help to create different effects

Dulce et Decorum Est (Pages 30-31)

1) The consonance of the 'k' sounds in the simile "coughing like hags" mimics the sound of a choking cough to emphasise how the young soldiers are suffering from illness due to war.

2) Onomatopoeic verbs (e.g."trudge") give the reader a sense of the soldiers' weariness.

Excerpt from 'The Prelude' (Pages 36-37)

1) Sibilance in "shod with steel, / We hiss'd along the polish'd ice" imitates the sound of ice skating, while onomatopoeia in the word "hiss'd" also hints at the joy they felt when skating.

2) The simile "every icy crag / Tinkled like iron" evokes the sound of bells and contrasts with the "village clock" that the narrator ignored — nature's sounds seem more captivating than those made by humans.

Poetic Devices

Irony can highlight the gap between expectations and reality

A Wife in London (Pages 20-21)

1) Hardy creates **irony** through the **different** speeds of **communication** — telegram and post — and how the wife is informed of her husband's death before she receives a letter from him.

2) Although the reader **expects** the devastating twist of events because the second part of the poem is called "**II — The Irony**", the wife doesn't. This makes us even more **sympathetic** to her heartbreak.

3) The **contrast** between the wife's **grief** and the husband's "<u>hoped return</u>" emphasises the painful irony.

Ozymandias (Pages 32-33)

1) 'Ozymandias' focuses on the irony that the king's **achievements** are ultimately **worthless** — all that's left of his kingdom is a **ruined statue**.

2) The **inscription** on the statue's base is ironic — the king warned others to "<u>despair</u>" when they saw his "<u>works</u>", but **none** of his **creations** are left now.

3) The irony also **challenges** the **reader** to consider their own view of **human achievement** — many people are similarly **blind** in their quest for **power**.

"Although I have no power left, you still have to learn about me... Ironic."

Poets appeal to the senses to create a vivid picture

London (Pages 6-7)

1) The poem is based around the scenes the speaker **sees** as he walks around the streets of London — the images of "<u>marks of woe</u>" on "<u>every face</u>", the "<u>black'ning Church</u>" and the "<u>blood</u>" that runs down "<u>Palace walls</u>" combine to create a picture of **pain**, **corruption** and **death**.

2) **Sounds** are also important — the combination of the "<u>Infant's cry of fear</u>", the "<u>Chimney-sweeper's cry</u>" and the "<u>youthful Harlot's curse</u>" create a noisy, **unpleasant impression** of the city.

Death of a Naturalist (Pages 22-23)

1) The poem uses lots of complex images that involve multiple senses all at once.

2) The narrator describes how "<u>bluebottles / Wove a strong gauze of sound around the smell</u>", using language of sight, touch, sound and smell to fully immerse the reader in the setting.

3) In the second stanza, the narrator's harmony with nature is broken, and the sensory language becomes more unsettling ("<u>blunt heads farting</u>"). By continuing to appeal to several senses, the narrator reveals that although nature is more or less the same, the narrator's attitude to nature has changed.

To Autumn (Pages 26-27)

1) Keats uses a particular type of **sensory language** in each **stanza** — the first centres on the sense of **touch**, the second on **sight**, and the last on **sound**, capturing **all aspects** of autumn's **abundance**.

2) The use of language related to sound in the last stanza creates a **mournful scene**. The "<u>wailful choir</u>" of gnats and the lambs' "<u>loud bleat</u>" remind the reader of autumn's **mortality** — it's slowly **dying**.

OTHER POEMS

You could also think about the use of contrasts...

Lots of the poems use contrasts for emphasis — oxymorons in 'London' show how even innocent things have been corrupted, while in 'Mametz Wood', the violent images of war contrast with human fragility.

Imagery

Imagery is language that creates a picture — it includes similes, metaphors and personification.

> 1) **Personification** can make things seem more **real** or **lifelike**.
>
> 2) **Similes** and **metaphors** create **powerful descriptions**.

Personification gives a vivid impression of an object or place

The Soldier (Pages 8-9)

1) England is personified as a woman who has given the soldier various gifts, including "<u>her flowers to love</u>" — the flowers could stand for England's countryside. The speaker could be implying that he owes England a debt of gratitude, and that he will repay her by fighting for his country.

2) England is even presented as a mother in that she "<u>bore</u>" his "<u>dust</u>". By associating England with **motherhood**, Brooke suggests she is **caring** and **protective** towards her people.

Mametz Wood (Pages 34-35)

1) The earth is personified to suggest it has **human feelings**. It is also described as having a "<u>wound</u>", which reflects how severely nature was affected by the fighting during **World War One**.

2) By describing how the earth "<u>stands sentinel</u>", Sheers draws a parallel between it and a **soldier**, reminding the reader of those who **died in the war**. He also suggests that the earth is **protecting** the **bones** of the soldiers and is taking an **active role** in allowing them to be **remembered**.

Similes and metaphors can be powerful ways of making a point

The Manhunt (Pages 2-3)

1) Metaphors to do with **inanimate objects** describe the man's **war-damaged body**. For example, the narrator refers to "**<u>the rungs of his broken ribs</u>**", emphasising the **dehumanising** nature of war.

2) The "<u>sweating, unexploded mine / buried deep in his mind</u>" is a metaphor that hints at the man's **distress** — it suggests war has left him with **unresolved emotional issues** that he still needs to tackle.

Valentine (Pages 18-19)

1) Duffy uses the onion as an extended metaphor for the narrator and her lover's relationship.

2) The simile "<u>like the careful undressing of love</u>" suggests that by accepting the metaphorical onion and thinking carefully about what it represents, the addressee will come to understand love better.

Dulce et Decorum Est (Pages 30-31)

1) The simile of the soldier "<u>flound'ring like a man in fire or lime</u>" shows how **damaging** the gas is, to the point where it makes the soldier writhe around **desperately** as if he'd do anything to escape it.

2) Owen uses the metaphor of a "<u>drowning</u>" man in a "<u>green sea</u>" to emphasise the **distress** caused by the gas attack. It **contrasts** with the **idealistic** portrayals of war seen in some other poems of the time.

Other poems also use personification...

Both Keats and Heaney personify nature in their poems — autumn is presented as a human worker in 'To Autumn', while in 'Death of a Naturalist', personification makes nature seem threatening.

Beginnings and Endings

Poets spend hours structuring their poems, so there's always plenty to analyse in the openings and endings.

1) The **beginning** of a poem usually **sets the tone** for the rest of the poem and **draws in the reader**.

2) Endings **round off** a poem — often leaving the reader with a **powerful** or **memorable** image.

Openings can be used to set the scene

Structure is the way that poets order and develop their ideas in a poem. The beginnings and endings of poems are key structural devices.

Death of a Naturalist (Pages 22-23)

1) The opening image of the flax dam which "<u>festered</u>" throughout the year uses language related to **rot** and **disease** to highlight the speaker's initial **fascination** with nature, and to establish the poem's **setting**.

2) This reference to **decay** sets up one of the poem's **main ideas** — it **foreshadows** the narrator's **realisation** that his childhood **fascination** with nature has **rotted** and died.

Afternoons (Pages 28-29)

1) The poem opens with the line "<u>Summer is fading</u>", which highlights that the seasons are changing, but also introduces the theme of loss — the **end** of summer often symbolises the death of living things.

2) The falling leaves could **represent** the **end** of youth. By having them "<u>fall in ones and twos</u>", Larkin suggests that change is gradual — it could be that the change in the women's lives goes unnoticed.

Ozymandias (Pages 32-33)

1) The opening line is the only time that the reader hears the **narrator's voice** — the rest of the poem is the **reported speech** of the "<u>traveller</u>".

2) This creates a **distance** between the **reader** and **Ozymandias** — the reader only hears a **second-hand account** about Ozymandias, reducing the **importance** of the ruler.

Paul feared that the ending might not be as fun as the beginning...

Last lines can leave you with doubts or round the poem off

The Manhunt (Pages 2-3)

1) The ending feels **unresolved** as the narrator recalls how she only came "<u>close</u>" to **reconnecting** with her husband. It leaves the reader with **doubt** as to whether she ever will **fully reconnect** with him.

2) This idea is emphasised through the way "<u>close</u>" almost **rhymes** with the previous line ("<u>closed</u>") — the poem's **fractured rhyme scheme** hints that war has **damaged** their sense of **togetherness**.

As Imperceptibly as Grief (Pages 14-15)

1) The extended metaphor of the changing of the seasons which symbolises the stages in the narrator's grieving process draws to a close in the final four lines when "<u>Summer made her light escape</u>".

2) The positive connotations of the final word of the poem, "<u>Beautiful</u>", reflect how, eventually, the end of grief is positive. This gives the poem's ending a sense of resolution.

OTHER POEMS

You could even comment on the titles of poems...

The vagueness of the title 'The Soldier' suggests that Brooke wanted his poem to feel relevant to any soldier, whereas the title of Duffy's 'Valentine' implies that the poem is a romantic note to someone.

Rhyme and Rhythm

Rejoice happily, your teacher has marshmallows — there's no excuse for spelling 'rhythm' wrong.

1) **Rhyme** and **rhythm** affect the **mood** of a poem and how it **flows**.
2) They can also be used to create a particular **effect**, or to emphasise the **message** of a poem.

Rhyme can reinforce a poem's message

London (Pages 6-7)

1) The regular ABAB rhyme scheme emphasises the unrelenting suffering and lack of change in the city.
2) The rhymes are simple and often monosyllabic (e.g. "street" and "meet"), creating a strong pulse. This could replicate the thudding sound of a heartbeat, presenting the city's people collectively as one.

Cozy Apologia (Pages 16-17)

1) 'Cozy Apologia' opens with **rhyming couplets** in the first stanza to **mimic** the **sentimentality** of the **romantic clichés**. The couplets are used **sarcastically** to show how the narrator **rejects** these clichés.
2) However, the rhyme scheme **breaks down** midway through the second stanza, upon the arrival of **Hurricane Floyd**, as if the hurricane is **distracting** her from thoughts of her partner.
3) In the final four lines, the rhyme scheme returns to a **more secure** ABAB pattern, which could reflect how the narrator embraces the **comfort** her relationship brings, even if it does involve **sentimentality**.

To Autumn (Pages 26-27)

1) Keats employs a varying rhyme scheme — the first stanza is ABABCDEDCCE and the second and third are ABABCDECDDE. This implies that autumn is a moving process, rather than a static event.
2) A couplet appears just before the end of each stanza and echoes a rhyme from earlier in the stanza, suggesting that the narrator is reminiscing, or reflecting on how they don't want autumn to pass.

A poem's rhythm affects its pace and mood

Afternoons (Pages 28-29)

1) The poem has **no fixed rhythm** and **varies** from line to line — this perhaps reflects the narrator's view that the people described have a **meaningless existence**.
2) Despite this, the **caesurae** make the pace fairly **soft** and **steady**. This could either reflect the **gentle rustling** of the autumn **leaves** or the **monotony** of the lives described.

Dulce et Decorum Est (Pages 30-31)

1) Owen's poem consists mainly of ten syllables per line. However, it doesn't follow iambic metre, which creates a broken, clumsy rhythm to reflect the fumbling of the soldiers in the gas attack.
2) Owen could be breaking away from the gentle, musical rhythms of other war poems, such as Brooke's 'The Soldier', to suggest that war is not as pleasant and honourable as it's sometimes made out to be.

Rhyme schemes are important in other poems...

'A Wife in London' has a regular ABBAB rhyme scheme which reflects the inevitability of death in war. In 'Ozymandias', the lack of a typical sonnet rhyme scheme reflects the destruction of human power.

Voice

The voice is a key feature of a poem — it can have a big effect on how the poet's message is conveyed.

1) A first-person voice gives you one person's **personal perspective**.
2) Third-person narrators are more **removed** from the action.

A first-person voice reveals the narrator's feelings or emotions

Sonnet 43 (Pages 4-5)

1) The first-person voice allows the reader to **listen in** on the speaker's **private** feelings about her lover.
2) Additionally, by using the **second-person** pronoun "<u>thee</u>", the reader becomes the **addressee** — the narrator's love is **projected** onto the reader, giving them a better sense of how **real** it is.

Hawk Roosting (Pages 24-25)

1) The hawk's arrogance is shown through first-person pronouns such as "<u>I</u>", "<u>me</u>" and "<u>my</u>" — these appear several times in the poem, showing how **self-important** and **possessive** the hawk is.
2) Hughes uses the first person to establish the hawk's **control** — it can present itself however it wishes to the reader **without being questioned**. It also reflects how the hawk will "<u>keep things like this</u>" — the hawk believes that no other animal or even God has any say in its reign.

Excerpt from 'The Prelude' (Pages 36-37)

1) The first-person voice **disappears** towards the end, reflecting how the speaker is **immersed** in nature.
2) The use of the first-person plural "<u>we</u>" in "<u>We hiss'd</u>" or "<u>we flew</u>" creates the sense that the narrator's "<u>rapture</u>" stemmed from how he went skating "<u>Confederate</u>" (in a group) **with others**.

Third-person narrators comment on what they see

A Wife in London (Pages 20-21)

1) The use of a third-person voice makes the poem less personal, suggesting that losing a husband at war wasn't an isolated experience — the wife symbolises the countless other widows across the country.
2) The detached narrator heightens the loneliness the wife feels after losing her husband, as the reader doesn't hear any of her feelings, suggesting that no one cares about her (or women like her).

Mametz Wood (Pages 34-35)

1) The **third-person voice** creates a **distance** between the narrator and the battlefield, allowing them to give a detached perspective on the **realities of war**. This makes it seem as though the narrator is conveying **fact**, rather than **opinion**, which makes the idea that the soldiers should be remembered **convincing**.
2) However, even though the poem is written in the third-person, the narrator is still **biased**. Describing a soldier's finger using the word "<u>relic</u>" shows that the narrator holds the **soldiers** and their **sacrifices** in **high esteem**, as 'relics' are body parts belonging to **saints**.

Poems can directly address someone or something...

The speaker in 'Valentine' speaks to their lover as they present them with an onion, symbolising their love, while the narrator of 'To Autumn' addresses a personification of autumn in an appreciative tone.

Mood

Sadly there are no teenage-angst poems in the anthology, but there's still plenty for you to write about moods.

> 1) The mood is the feeling or atmosphere created in a poem.
>
> 2) Poets often change the mood of the poem as it progresses.

Language can be used to create a specific mood

The Soldier (Pages 8-9)

1) Natural images of "flowers" and "rivers" create a blissful mood — they emphasise England's beauty to the point where it is compared to a "heaven" on Earth.

2) Religious language is used to create a hopeful mood which might help comfort the soldiers and their families. The repetition of "dust" is reminiscent of the funeral passage "ashes to ashes, dust to dust", suggesting that although the soldiers' bodies may be buried, their souls will go to heaven.

A Wife in London (Pages 20-21)

1) The "tawny vapour" creates a bleak mood, while the simile "Like a waning taper" foreshadows the bad news — the wife soon learns that her husband's life has been extinguished like the candle.

2) Hardy never mentions death or war explicitly — he uses the word "fallen" euphemistically, and refers vaguely to the war in the "far South Land". These indirect references create a sombre mood. The upbeat tone of the husband's letter in the final stanza emphasises the mournful mood by highlighting how his promising future has been cut short.

Some poems have a change in mood

Living Space (Pages 12-13)

1) A serious mood is created at the start through the use of language that has negative connotations (e.g. "problem", "Nothing", "dangerously").

2) However, the mood becomes more hopeful when the reader learns that there is a "living space" in the ramshackle building.

3) The "eggs in a wire basket" add to this hopeful mood, as eggs can be seen to symbolise new life, suggesting the inhabitants' lives may improve.

"But I thought you liked puns."
"Nah, I'm just not in the mood."

Cozy Apologia (Pages 16-17)

1) The first stanza is full of romantic clichés, such as the "hero" on a "dappled mare" who wears "chain mail". These create a sentimental mood, although the reader also gets the impression that the narrator is being slightly tongue-in-cheek.

2) The romantic mood is broken at the start of the second stanza when the hurricane arrives. The hyphenation of "post-post-modern" and "do-it-now-and-take-no-risks" creates a disordered mood to reflect the disruptive nature of the hurricane as well as the narrator's fleeting relationships.

3) The word "bunkered" gives a sense of security in the final stanza and reflects the couple's cosiness.

Duffy's 'Valentine' also has a shift in mood...

The relaxed, affectionate mood created when the narrator presents the onion gradually becomes more intense — the poem ends on the word "knife". This change in mood compares well with 'Cozy Apologia'.

Practice Questions

It's the end of the section and yep, you guessed it — time for some practice questions to check you've taken everything in. You can always look back at the poems to help you answer each question...

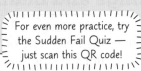

For even more practice, try the Sudden Fail Quiz — just scan this QR code!

Sudden Fail Quiz

Forms of Poetry

1) Comment on the form of 'Sonnet 43'. Why might the poet have chosen this form?

2) Explain how the form of 'She Walks in Beauty' is used to illustrate the woman's attractiveness.

3) Why do you think Dharker chose an irregular form for 'Living Space'? Explain your answer.

4) In 'Valentine', how does Duffy use form to present the narrator's emotions?

Poetic Devices

1) Find a technique in 'Hawk Roosting' that conveys the hawk's power and explain how it does this.

2) How does the narrator of 'Sonnet 43' use anaphora to highlight her ideas?

3) What effect do repeated sounds have in 'Dulce et Decorum Est'?

4) How do sound devices help to convey the narrator's feelings in the excerpt from 'The Prelude'?

> Shall I compare thee to a summer's day?

5) Part of 'A Wife in London' is called "II – The Irony". Why do you think Hardy gave this part of the poem this title?

6) Explain how Blake creates a vivid representation of the city in 'London'.

7) In 'Death of a Naturalist', how does Heaney bring the flax dam setting to life for the reader?

8) How does Keats use sound to imply that autumn is fading away in the last stanza of 'To Autumn'?

Imagery

1) Do you think the use of personification is more effective in 'The Soldier' or 'Mametz Wood'? Explain your answer.

2) Find an example of imagery used in 'The Manhunt' to describe the soldier's body. Explain the meaning and significance of the image.

3) How is imagery used in 'Valentine' to present the complicated nature of love?

4) How does Owen use imagery to convey the dying soldier's pain in 'Dulce et Decorum Est'?

Practice Questions

Beginnings and Endings

'And they all lived happily ever after.' Hmm, not in this poetry collection.

1) How does the beginning of 'Death of a Naturalist' reflect both sides of the narrator's feelings towards nature? Explain your answer.

2) What does the beginning of 'Afternoons' imply about the lives led by the women in the poem?

3) Why do you think Shelley made the start of 'Ozymandias' different from the rest of the poem?

4) What does the ending of 'As Imperceptibly as Grief' suggest about the narrator's feelings?

Rhyme and Rhythm

1) Explain how Blake uses rhyme in 'London' to help convey the poem's message.

2) How does the rhyme scheme in 'Cozy Apologia' reflect the narrator's feelings about love?

3) What effect do the caesurae create in 'Afternoons'?

4) Do you think Owen's choice of rhythm in 'Dulce et Decorum Est' is effective? Explain your answer.

Voice

1) Why might a reader feel as if the narrator is speaking directly to them in 'Sonnet 43'?

2) In 'Hawk Roosting', does the use of the hawk's point of view add to or lessen the sense of the hawk's power? Explain your answer.

3) Why do you think Hardy chose to write 'A Wife in London' in the third person rather than the first person? Explain your answer.

4) How does the use of the third person in 'Mametz Wood' contribute to the poem's portrayal of war?

Mood

1) How might the mood of 'The Soldier' have affected people when it was first written?

2) How does Hardy create a sombre mood in 'A Wife in London'?

3) Would you say the mood in 'Living Space' is more serious or more hopeful? Explain your answer.

4) There is a mood change in 'Cozy Apologia'. Explain this change and its effect.

Practice Questions

Here's your third and final batch of exam-style questions. Sections Four, Five and Six have lots of advice about writing great exam answers, so have a read of those pages if you're looking for some hints and tips.

You should discuss the form, structure and language used by the poets and the effects that these create in both parts of the question. It's also important that you include relevant information about the context surrounding the poems — you could discuss how historical events or culture may have influenced the poet.

Exam-style Questions

1. i) There is a change in mood during Dharker's poem 'Living Space'.
       Discuss how Dharker creates and uses mood in the poem.

    ii) From the anthology, select another poem in which the mood is important. Compare how mood is created and used in 'Living Space' and the way it is created and used in your selected poem.

2. i) Shelley uses irony to present Ozymandias's loss of power.
       Explain how Shelley uses irony in the poem.

    ii) Select another poem from the anthology which also uses irony. Compare how irony is used in 'Ozymandias' and the way it is used in the poem you have chosen.

3. i) The narrator in Blake's 'London' is frustrated with the situation he sees in the city.
       Discuss how Blake conveys the narrator's frustration in the poem.

    ii) From the anthology, pick another poem which features a critical narrator. Compare how the narrator's criticism is shown in 'London' and the way it is shown in your selected poem.

4. i) Dickinson examines changing emotions in 'As Imperceptibly as Grief'.
       Discuss how Dickinson presents changing emotions in the poem.

    ii) Pick another poem from the anthology. Compare how changing emotions are presented in 'As Imperceptibly as Grief' and the way they are presented in the poem you have selected.

5. i) Byron shows that the speaker in 'She Walks in Beauty' worships the woman he describes.
       Explain how Byron presents this form of worship in the poem.

    ii) Select another poem from the anthology which features worship. Compare how worship is conveyed in 'She Walks in Beauty' and the way it is conveyed in the poem you have chosen.

6. i) The narrator of 'To Autumn' explores ideas about life and death.
       Examine how Keats presents ideas about life and death through the poem.

    ii) Pick another poem from the anthology which explores life and death. Compare how life and death are presented in 'To Autumn' and the way they are presented in your selected poem.

The Poetry Exam

If you're doing WJEC Eduqas English Literature, you'll have to sit two exams —
this book will help you prepare for the Poetry Anthology section of Component 1.

This is how your Component 1 exam will work

1) The Component 1 exam lasts for **2 hours**. It will be split into **two sections**, like this:

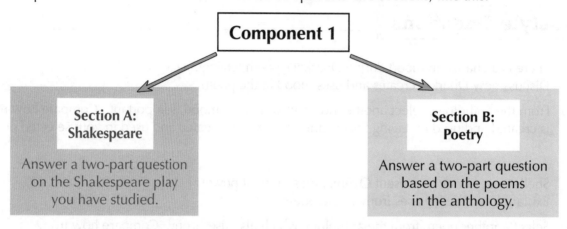

Component 1

Section A:
Shakespeare

Answer a two-part question
on the Shakespeare play
you have studied.

Section B:
Poetry

Answer a two-part question
based on the poems
in the anthology.

2) The next few pages give you **tips** on how to answer the question in **Section B**.

3) The question has **two parts**. The **first part** will test you on **one poem** from the anthology. The **second part** is a **comparison question** and will ask you to **compare** a poem with **any other poem** from the anthology.

4) **Section B** is worth **40 marks** — **20%** of your **entire GCSE**. You should spend about **one hour** on Section B, with roughly **20 minutes** of that spent on the **first part** and about **40 minutes** on the **second**.

5) You're **not allowed** to take your own anthology or any **notes** about the poems into the exam.

Read the question carefully and underline key words

1) Read the question for Section B carefully. Underline the **theme** and any other **key words**.

2) The **first part** will give you **one poem** and ask you to write about an **idea** or **theme**. It's worth **15 marks**.

3) Here's what the **first part of the question** might look like in the exam:

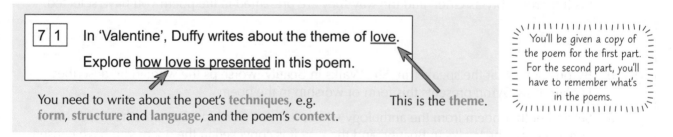

| 7 | 1 | In 'Valentine', Duffy writes about the theme of <u>love</u>. |

Explore <u>how love is presented</u> in this poem.

You need to write about the poet's **techniques**, e.g. **form**, **structure** and **language**, and the poem's **context**.

This is the **theme**.

You'll be given a copy of
the poem for the first part.
For the second part, you'll
have to remember what's
in the poems.

4) The **second part** will ask you to choose **another poem** from the anthology that shares the **same theme** as the poem from the first part. You will then have to **compare** the **presentation of this theme** in both poems.

5) The **second part** is worth **25 marks**. Here's what it might look like in the exam:

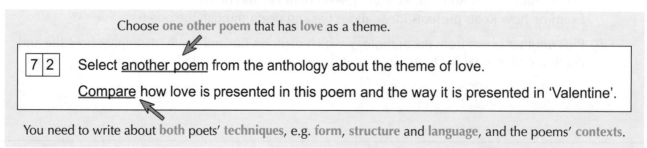

Choose **one other poem** that has **love** as a theme.

| 7 | 2 | Select <u>another poem</u> from the anthology about the theme of love. |

Compare how love is presented in this poem and the way it is presented in 'Valentine'.

You need to write about **both** poets' **techniques**, e.g. **form**, **structure** and **language**, and the poems' **contexts**.

How to Structure Your Answers

A solid structure is essential — it lets the examiner follow your argument nice and easily. Think about each essay like a sandwich — you need a tasty filling, sandwiched between an introduction and conclusion. Yum...

Start with an introduction and end with a conclusion

1) Your introduction to each part should begin by clearly laying out your argument in a sentence or two. In your answer to the second part, mention both of the poems you are going to write about.

2) Use the rest of the introduction to give a brief overview of how the poem or poems present the theme given in the question — include the main ideas from your plan (see p.74), but save the evidence for later.

3) The main body of each essay should be roughly three to five paragraphs that develop your argument.

4) Finish each essay with a conclusion — this should summarise your answer to the question. It's also your last chance to impress the examiner, so try to make your final sentence memorable.

Choose an appropriate second poem

1) Before you can answer the second part, you need to select another poem to compare with the poem given in the question.

Look over Section 2 for poems that share the same themes and might pair well together.

2) Choose a poem that's relevant to the theme given in the question and pairs well with the first poem.

3) For example, if the question asks you about anger in 'London', you could compare it to 'Dulce et Decorum Est' — both poems explore the anger felt over the waste of people's lives.

4) To help you select an appropriate poem, create groups of poems with similar themes when you revise.

In the second part, compare the poems in every paragraph

1) In each paragraph of the main body, write about one poem and then explain how the other poem is similar or different.

Make sure you write about both poems equally — you could lose marks if you focus too much on one of the poems.

2) Every paragraph should compare a feature of the poems, such as their form, their structure, the language they use or the feelings they put across.

3) Remember to start a new paragraph every time you start comparing a new feature.

4) You should use a range of linking words or phrases to signpost your argument and vary your writing:

To show similarities:	
• similarly	• in the same way
• likewise	• equally

To show differences:	
• whereas	• in contrast
• however	• on the other hand

There are three main ways to get marks

There are three main things to keep in mind when you're planning and writing each answer:

- Give your own thoughts and opinions on the poems and support them with quotes from the text.
- Explain features like form, structure and language.
- Describe the similarities and differences between poems and their contexts.

How to Structure Your Answers

The exam is no time to discover your inner politician — you actually need to answer the question you're given.

Use P.E.E.D. to structure each paragraph

1) **P.E.E.D.** stands for: **P**oint, **E**xample, **E**xplain, **D**evelop.

> In the second part, after you've explained your first example, give an example from the other poem and explain that too.

POINT — Begin each paragraph by making a **point**.

EXAMPLE — Then give an **example** from the poem.

EXPLAIN — Explain **how** the example **supports** your opening point.

DEVELOP — Finish the paragraph by **developing** your point further. See below for ways to do this.

2) This is just a **framework** to make sure your paragraphs have all the **features** they need to pick up marks — you **don't** have to follow it **rigidly** in **every** paragraph.

3) Here's an **example** of how you could use **P.E.E.D.** to structure a paragraph for the second part:

Give <u>examples</u> from one or both of the poems.

Develop your point — for example, by writing about the effect on the reader.

Start by making a <u>point</u> to support your argument.

Explain how the examples relate to your opening point.

'Valentine' and 'Cozy Apologia' both reject traditional images of love. Duffy's statement "Not a red rose" in the opening line suggests that the narrator sees stereotypical symbols of love as lacking meaning. Similarly, the speaker in 'Cozy Apologia' chooses to link her partner with the domestic imagery of a "lamp" and a "pen", hinting that traditional symbols are not an accurate reflection of her own relationship. In both poems, the rejection of conventional images of love challenges the idealised relationships that they are usually associated with, instead highlighting the ordinary, often complex, nature of real relationships.

Develop each of your points

You can develop your points in a **variety** of ways — here are some ideas:

- **Explain** the **effect** on the reader.
- **Analyse** the **language** more closely.
- **Link** to some relevant **context**.
- **Link** to **another part** of the poem.
- Give an **alternative interpretation** of your example.

Link each paragraph to the question

1) Your points should be **linked** to the question and follow a **clear** central **argument**.

2) A good way to make sure your points all follow a central argument is to start each paragraph with an **opening statement** that directly connects back to the question. Here's an **example**:

Write about the way loss is presented in 'As Imperceptibly as Grief'.

The theme of the question is 'loss'.

'As Imperceptibly as Grief' uses the imagery of the changing seasons to explore the sense of loss that is felt when the grieving process comes to an end.

Start each paragraph by linking the poem (or poems) to the theme.

Commenting on Poetic Techniques

You can't just talk about *what* the poem says — you need to explain *how* and *why* the poet has chosen to write the poem in a certain way. It's like being a detective, but maybe a little less exciting. Only a smidge.

You should comment on language

1) Analyse the **language** — think about **why** the poet has used certain **words** and **language techniques**.

2) Make sure you **comment** on the **effect** that the poem's language has on the reader. The examiner wants to know how the poem makes you **feel**.

There is more on language techniques on pages 58-60.

3) This is the kind of thing you could write about **language**:

> 'The Manhunt' uses a combination of violent sounds and language of fragility to convey the man's broken state. The metaphor of the "parachute silk of his punctured lung" uses alliteration of the plosive 'p' sound to add a stabbing force to the phrase, emphasising how his lung has been damaged in the war. The man's fragility is reinforced through the use of the delicate material "silk", which could suggest that he is weaker than he was, or that humans are not designed to be placed in such dangerous situations. The descriptions of the soldier's body as a series of individual, damaged body parts further emphasises the soldier's broken state.

Analyse the effects of key quotes.

Always develop your ideas.

Mention form and structure when it's relevant

1) As well as language, you could analyse the **form** and **structure** of the poems.

2) **Form** refers to features such as the **type of poem**, number of lines, **rhyme scheme** and **rhythm**, whereas **structure** is about **how ideas progress** through the poem.

There is more on form on page 57 and structure on page 61.

3) The examiner will be **impressed** by analysis of form and structure, but only if it's **relevant** to your point. You should explain **why** a particular aspect of form or structure has been used and link it to the **theme**.

4) Make sure your analysis of structure and form is **integrated** into the rest of your essay — don't just mention it at the end as an afterthought. Here's an **example** of how to write about a poem's form:

> Brooke uses the poetic form of 'The Soldier' to emphasise the narrator's patriotic love for his country. 'The Soldier' is a sonnet, a form traditionally used for love poetry, so its use here reinforces the strength of the speaker's emotions towards England. Brooke's use of a regular rhyme scheme highlights this love by creating a sense of order and stability, which reflects the sense of comfort England brings. It is the narrator's love of his home country that comforts him in the face of the chaos of the war.

Link the form of the poem directly to your argument.

Give additional details about form to reinforce your point.

Use literary language

1) Your writing should be **sophisticated**, **concise** and **accurate**, with no vague words or waffle.

2) It should show an **impressive range** of **vocabulary**. **Vary** the **words** you use to write about **key themes** in the poems, e.g. instead of repeating 'love', you could say 'feelings', 'affection' or 'devotion'.

3) To get top marks, you need to use the **correct technical terms** when you're writing about poetry, e.g. 'metaphors' or 'onomatopoeia' — there's a handy **glossary** at the back of this book to **explain** these terms.

4) However, make sure you **only** use words that you know the **meaning** of. For example, don't say that a poem has a '**volta**' if you don't know what it **really means** — it will be **obvious** to the examiner.

Using Evidence

Quotes and references go a long way to support your answer — here's a handy guide to the dos and don'ts.

Memorise useful quotes for the exam

1) As well as knowing the poems inside out, it's really **important** to **learn quotes** that you can use in the exam. Make yourself a **bank** of quotes and examples from each poem that you can use to **support** your answers.

2) Learn quotes that are **relevant** to specific **themes** — exam questions generally focus on these.

3) Keep your quotes **as short as possible** — **cut out** anything **unnecessary**. This will make them **easier to remember** and you'll spend **less time** writing them out in the exam.

Use details from the text to back up your points

1) You need to back up your ideas with quotes from or references to the text.

2) Choose your quotes carefully — they have to be relevant to the point you're making.

3) Don't quote large chunks of text — instead, use short quotes and embed them in your sentences.

✗ Hughes's poem suggests that all aspects of nature are perfectly suited to the hawk's hunting — "The convenience of the high trees! / The air's buoyancy and the sun's ray / Are of advantage to me".

> This quote is too long and it doesn't fit into the sentence structure.

✓ In 'Hawk Roosting', Hughes emphasises the hawk's self-importance by describing how it believes the "sun is behind" it and that nature is "of advantage" to it.

> These quotes are nicely embedded into the sentence.

4) Quotes are usually the clearest way to illustrate a point, but sometimes you can use a paraphrased detail instead — e.g. if you need to describe one of the writer's techniques, or one of the text's features.

5) Don't just write a lengthy explanation of what's going on in the poem — like quotes, keep any references brief and relevant to your argument.

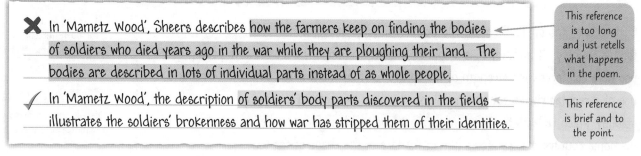

✗ In 'Mametz Wood', Sheers describes how the farmers keep on finding the bodies of soldiers who died years ago in the war while they are ploughing their land. The bodies are described in lots of individual parts instead of as whole people.

> This reference is too long and just retells what happens in the poem.

✓ In 'Mametz Wood', the description of soldiers' body parts discovered in the fields illustrates the soldiers' brokenness and how war has stripped them of their identities.

> This reference is brief and to the point.

6) Don't forget to explain your quotes — you need to use them as evidence to support your argument.

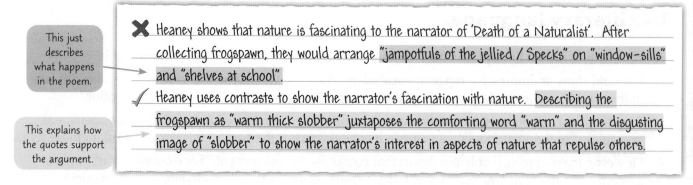

> This just describes what happens in the poem.

✗ Heaney shows that nature is fascinating to the narrator of 'Death of a Naturalist'. After collecting frogspawn, they would arrange "jampotfuls of the jellied / Specks" on "window-sills" and "shelves at school".

✓ Heaney uses contrasts to show the narrator's fascination with nature. Describing the frogspawn as "warm thick slobber" juxtaposes the comforting word "warm" and the disgusting image of "slobber" to show the narrator's interest in aspects of nature that repulse others.

> This explains how the quotes support the argument.

Writing About Context

It might be tempting to swallow a history book so that you can impress the examiner with all your knowledge, but don't bother (also, it hurts). Adding context is about linking the poems to big ideas, *not* regurgitating facts.

Use relevant context to show wider knowledge

1) You should use context to show that you have some broader knowledge of the poems.

2) Using context can be tricky to get right — the examiners want to see that you understand big ideas such as patriotism and guilt, not that you can reel off lots of historical facts and biographical details.

3) Here's a list of dos and don'ts for how to use context in your answer:

Do
1) Use brief, relevant context to help you explain or develop a point.
2) Clearly link context back to your argument.
3) Integrate context into your analysis of language, form and structure.
4) Show an understanding of the broad theme mentioned in the question, e.g. worship.

Don't
1) Add irrelevant historical facts — this will waste time and won't get you any marks.
2) Include irrelevant biographical details about the poet that aren't linked to your argument.
3) Tack context onto the end of a paragraph without linking it to your point.
4) Allow context to dominate your essay — it shouldn't be the main subject of your points.

4) Here's an example of how not to use context in your answer:

> ✗ Elizabeth Barrett Browning was born in 1806. She was a popular Victorian poet and 'Sonnet 43' is one of the poems that she is best remembered for.

Neither of these facts are linked to a point or support an argument.

This date is irrelevant.

5) Here are a couple of good examples of how you could use context in your answer:

> ✓ In 'A Wife in London', the "far South Land" where the husband "has fallen" could refer to South Africa, where the Boer War was being fought when the poem was written. Due to its implicit link between war and death, Hardy's poem could be perceived to be an anti-war one.

Use brief, relevant context to show wider knowledge.

Link context to the question theme ('war') to develop your argument.

> ✓ In 'Afternoons', Larkin explores the nature of identity. By describing the women in the poem only as "Young mothers", the speaker suggests that this is all they are. This could reflect the gender roles that were prevalent in the 1960s when the poem was written: women were often expected to stay at home to raise their children. Larkin could therefore be hinting at the frustration caused by the restrictive nature of gender roles, an issue which resonates with people across different time periods and cultures as they try to establish their own identities.

Clearly link point to the theme of the question ('identity').

You can use a universal idea or experience, such as gender roles, as context.

Planning Your Answers

In an exam, it's always tempting to launch straight into writing your answers, but that can end in disaster. Making a plan is the key to a sophisticated, well-structured essay. Trust me — it's worth it.

In the exam, spend five minutes planning your answers

1) Always **plan** your answers **before** you start writing so that you're less likely to forget something **important**.

2) Write your plans at the **top of your answer booklet** and draw a **line** through them when you've finished.

3) **Don't** spend **too long** on your plans. It's only **rough work**, so you don't need to write in full sentences. Here are a few **examples** of different ways you can plan your answers:

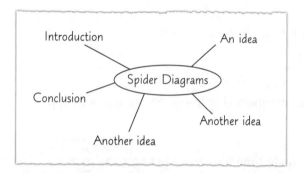

Bullet points with...
- Intro...
- An idea...
- The next idea...

Tables with...

A point...	Quote to back this up...
Another point...	Quote...
A different point...	Quote...

4) A good plan will help you **organise** your ideas — and write a good, **well-structured** essay.

Here's a sample question and plan

> | 7 | 2 | Select another poem from the anthology which features a proud character.
>
> Compare how pride is presented in this poem and the way it is presented in 'Ozymandias'.

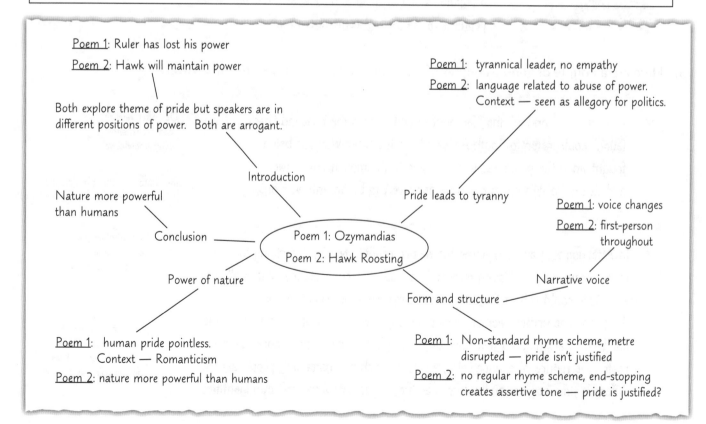

Sample Answer

Here's how you could use the plan on page 74 to write a really good answer.

Compare the poems in your opening sentence.

Both 'Ozymandias' and 'Hawk Roosting' explore the idea of pride but through two different dominant figures — the first through the ancient king Ozymandias (the Greek name for the Egyptian pharaoh Ramesses II), and the second through a hawk perched in the woods. However, while both poems portray their central figures as proud, Ozymandias has lost his power to nature and time, whereas the hawk intends to maintain its control. The poems suggest that too much pride is damaging, but also that human pride in particular is pointless since nature is so much more powerful than mankind.

Sum up the main argument of your essay.

The figures in both poems are presented as tyrants whose pride makes them abusive. In 'Ozymandias', the king's tyranny is implied through his "sneer of cold command". The adjective "cold" implies a lack of empathy, while the harsh alliteration in "cold command" suggests the king would give out orders without emotion. Furthermore, the word "sneer" suggests a lack of respect for his people, as if his pride made him feel superior to them. The reader of 'Hawk Roosting' is encouraged to view pride in a similarly negative light. When the hawk says "I kill where I please because it is all mine", its use of simple, mostly monosyllabic language and the lack of contractions (the hawk uses "it is" rather than "it's") makes its voice sound robotic, suggesting that its pride makes it unemotional about subjecting others to pain. The hawk therefore shares the same cruel human traits that Ozymandias exhibits; this comes across so strongly that when the poem was first published, some speculated that 'Hawk Roosting' was an allegory for the way political dictators persecute their people.

Try to develop your ideas.

Discuss the language used in the two poems.

Suggest more than one interpretation of the poem.

Each poem's use of narrative voice reveals something about the relationship between the central character's pride and their level of power. 'Ozymandias' is structured as a layered narrative consisting of three voices — the person who spoke to the traveller, the traveller and Ozymandias. Ozymandias's voice is therefore buried deep within the poem, mimicking the way his statue is obscured by the sand. Ozymandias's lack of power over his own poem makes his proud, hyperbolic declaration that he is "king of kings" seem foolish. In contrast, 'Hawk Roosting' is written in the first person throughout, which reflects the hawk's power and control; the hawk can present itself as it wishes. As there are no other voices in the poem to confirm or challenge the hawk's sense of superiority, the reader has no choice but to accept that its pride is justified.

Focus on a different feature in each paragraph, e.g. narrative voice.

Compare the poems' use of form.

Give a personal response to the poems.

This answer continues on page 76.

Sample Answer

Aspects of form reinforce the idea that Ozymandias's pride is less legitimate than the hawk's. Shelley uses the sonnet form, but doesn't follow the traditional sonnet rhyme scheme, while the breakdown of form implied through half-rhymes such as "appear" and "despair" reflects the erosion of the statue and of Ozymandias's power. Additionally, the poem is written mostly in iambic pentameter, but it is often disrupted, as if Ozymandias's power is unstable or under threat. 'Hawk Roosting', however, is written in free verse without a fixed rhyme scheme, but the lines are concise and even, which gives the reader the impression that the hawk has control over the poem's form. The rhyming couplet "feet" and "eat" in the first stanza reinforces how "perfect" its kills are, suggesting that its pride in its ruthlessness is well-founded.

Even though the hawk's power appears to be justified, the figures in both poems hint at the pointlessness of human pride more generally. In 'Ozymandias', the "shattered visage" of the statue lies "Half sunk" in the sand. The words "shattered" and "Half" have connotations of incompleteness, suggesting that nature can damage and obscure human works. Additionally, the desert is "boundless and bare", showing how nature dwarfs everything else and is able to outlast any aspect of human life. Shelley was a key figure in the English Romantic movement, which put emphasis on the power of nature, so by ending the poem with the natural environment, he reinforces the powerlessness of humans. In 'Hawk Roosting', however, the hawk is part of nature. The hawk's position at the "top of the wood" symbolises its absolute power over the Earth, while its claim that it holds "Creation" in its "foot", implies that the natural world (represented by the hawk) has control over everything, including humans and gods. If this is true, the reader must conclude that human pride, such as that displayed by Ozymandias, is misplaced — nature is a timeless and dominant force that will always eclipse any form of human power.

Both 'Ozymandias' and 'Hawk Roosting' present characters who proudly believe themselves to be powerful. Both are arrogant, in that they exhibit excessive pride to the point where they believe that their power gives them the right to treat others poorly. It is only Ozymandias who is seemingly punished for his pride, as his statue disintegrates and people no longer remember him as a mighty ruler. Even though the hawk maintains its power, the fact that it is a part of the natural world hints at the power of nature over humanity. In this sense, the two poems could be suggesting that nature is the most powerful force on Earth, making human pride ultimately laughable.

Use the correct technical terms.

Start each paragraph with a clear opening statement that links to the question.

Use the conclusion to summarise your answer and link it to the terms used in the question.

Use linking words to signpost comparisons.

Use quotes to support your argument.

Explain the effect of the examples you give.

Bring in some relevant contextual details to your answer to show wider understanding.

Your last sentence should sum up your argument, and it needs to be memorable.

Exam Tips

We've scoured examiners' reports and mark schemes, and distilled them all into this dazzling page of top tips — that was one wild weekend. Here's a whistle-stop tour of what you should and shouldn't do to ace the exam.

Here are our top 10 things to do in the exam...

1) **Do** make sure you **know the poems** really well before you go into the exam.

2) **Do** come up with your own **interpretations** of the poems that can be **supported** with evidence.

3) **Do read and reread** the poem you're given really carefully, and check that you're **quoting** from it correctly in your answers.

4) **Do** choose a suitable poem in the second part to **compare** to the one you're given — it needs to link clearly to the **theme** in the question.

5) **Do plan** your answers. Plans help you **organise** your thoughts and give clear responses.

6) **Do** remember to comment on **structure** and **form** as well as language.

7) **Do** write about **why** the poet **chose** to use particular **words** and **techniques** — think about the **effects** they may have been trying to create.

> The poet used a full stop because... it was the end of a sentence. Ooh yeah, that's good.

8) **Do** remember to write about the **context** of the poems. Make sure the context is **relevant** to your point and **clearly linked** to the question.

9) **Do** use **short quotes** from the poems to **save time** and make your answer **clear**.

10) **Do** compare the poems in part two — you should write a roughly **equal amount** about each one.

... and here are our top 10 things not to do

1) Don't just rewrite an essay that you've written before the exam — it might not be answering the question properly and the points you make might not be relevant.

2) Don't answer the question that you wish had been asked — make sure you answer the question that has been asked.

3) Don't just name the techniques being used — you need to explain the effect they have too.

4) Don't jump straight into answering the question without planning.

5) Don't contradict yourself or change your mind halfway through — this can make your points seem weak. It's fine to discuss two sides of an argument, but you need to come to a clear conclusion at the end.

6) Don't write your answer to the second part about just one of the poems — discuss them both fully.

7) Don't write about quotes in a way that misinterprets what they mean in the text, and don't shoehorn them in when they don't fit your argument. This will make it seem like you don't understand the poem.

8) Don't try to hide from the examiner by disguising yourself as a football — you may be kicked out.

9) Don't cram loads of points into each paragraph — stick to a structure like P.E.E.D. instead (see p.70).

10) Don't include unnecessary context if it doesn't link to the question or your argument.

Targeting Grade 8-9

Getting a top grade is a tricky old thing, but these pages will give you some pointers on how you can reach the dizzy heights of grade 9 — you're welcome.* *In the event that you get a grade 9, I accept thank you cards.

Know what the examiner wants

1) There's no single way to get a grade 9, but one of the most important things is to know what the examiner is looking for — aka the assessment objectives (AOs).

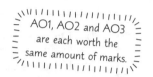

AO1, AO2 and AO3 are each worth the same amount of marks.

2) The table below shows how to meet the assessment objectives in the exam. You need to fulfil each of these objectives to get top marks.

Assessment Objective	What you need to do
AO1	• show a critical, insightful and engaged personal response to the poems • write highly coherent responses that clearly answer the questions • support arguments with well-integrated, relevant and precise examples from the poems
AO2	• analyse how the poets use language, form and structure, using relevant subject terminology to express your ideas • closely and perceptively explore how the poets create meaning and affect the reader
AO3	• give a detailed, relevant explanation of the relationship between the poems and their context

3) A good way to boost your marks is to identify objectives you struggle with and try to improve them.

4) Bear the AOs in mind when writing your answers, but don't treat them like a checklist that you need to tick off. Instead, you should use them to help shape your answers.

5) The next few pages show you how to use your understanding of the AOs to achieve a top grade.

Respond to the poems critically

1) Being critical means giving your own opinions about the poems.

2) The examiner wants to hear a personal response to the poems — write about how certain words, phrases or images make you feel and why they have that effect. Here's an example of how to do it:

> The adjective "miraculous" evokes a sense of wonder that the building is still standing. The reader is left in awe of the people who are able to survive in such precarious conditions.

3) In the second part, you could use your comparison of the poems to reach a judgement. For example, you could argue that one poem demonstrates an idea more strongly than the other or that one of the poems presents the question theme more positively than the other.

4) This can be an impressive way to conclude your answer. For example:

> 'A Wife in London' and 'Dulce et Decorum Est' can both be considered anti-war poems, each highlighting the terrible waste of life that war causes. It is Owen, however, who evokes a stronger emotional response in the reader. His vivid depiction of the gas attack and the dehumanised victim confronts the reader with the horrifying realities of war, revealing its futility and dismantling the patriotic propaganda that convinces young men to fight for their country.

Targeting Grade 8-9

Analyse the poems in depth

1) **Don't** just comment on the **surface meaning** of the poems, look out for lines which might have a **deeper significance**. Exploring these examples will make your analysis more **complex** and **thoughtful**.

> Byron's final line, "A heart whose love is innocent!", stresses the purity of the woman's character. However, concluding the poem in this way could also suggest that the narrator, despite his sustained focus on the woman's appearance, has little interest in a physical relationship and simply prefers to admire her beauty.

2) You should show you're aware that poems can be **interpreted** in **more than one** way.

3) If a poem is a bit **ambiguous**, or you think that a particular line or phrase could have several **different meanings**, then **say so**.

> In 'London', a reader could interpret the "youthful Harlot's curse" as a sexually transmitted disease, or to mean that prostitutes are a curse on the city. The "curse" first "Blasts the new born Infant's tear", which could suggest that the newborn child has been infected with the disease. It also "blights" a "Marriage hearse", hinting that marriage is equivalent to a death sentence; the disease spreads from the prostitute to her client, who passes it on to his new wife, whose death therefore seems inevitable.

4) You could also use **context** to come up with **alternative interpretations** that deepen your argument.

> The third stanza of 'To Autumn' has a more melancholy tone than the rest of the poem, as the narrator senses that the "soft-dying day" of autumn signals the approach of winter. Although the poem celebrates the power and abundance of nature, this final stanza recognises the inevitability of death in nature. However, the fact that 'To Autumn' was one of the final poems Keats wrote before his death from tuberculosis could suggest this sense of sadness at the certainty of death may also reflect an awareness of his own mortality.

Be original and insightful

1) The examiner will be **impressed** if you can come up with your own **original ideas** to answer the questions.

2) This **shows** that you've **really thought** about the poems and makes your answers **stand out** from the crowd.

3) Here are some **top tips** for how to be original:

- **Know** the poems **really well**.
- **Use** the information in this **book** as a **foundation** for your arguments, but make sure you **develop** your points with a **personal response** — one that can't be found in a revision guide.
- Do **your own research** into the poems' **contexts** — this might help you view the poems differently.
- Answer **practice questions** — they can help you come up with fresh ideas about the poems.
- Practise **pairing different combinations** of poems together. **Comparing** poems helps highlight different features in the individual poems and can help you come up with **original insights**.
- Focus on **really answering the questions** in the exam. Rather than using pre-prepared points, **think** about what the **questions** are asking, then use them to guide your thoughts about the poems.

Targeting Grade 8-9

Consider the structure of your essays

Pages 69-70 cover he essentials about structuring an essay, but you can boost your marks by **thinking carefully** about the best possible way to **order** your **ideas** and **structure** your **argument**.

Do

1) Integrate your analysis of poetic techniques into an analysis of the question's theme.

2) Pursue a clear argument throughout each essay — briefly outline this argument in your introduction, then link every paragraph to your argument.

3) Focus your comparison of the poems on a specific idea or attitude — e.g. if the questions asks you to write about 'change', you could focus your argument on the idea that change is inevitable.

Don't

1) Write about the poems **chronologically** (from their beginning to end) or follow a **rigid structure** of analysing language, then structure, then form — this will **prevent** you from going into real **depth**.

2) **Stick rigidly** to the P.E.E.D. structure if you don't want to — but you still need to make sure to **cover all** of these **aspects** (point, example, explain, develop) in each of your paragraphs.

Think about each poem as a deliberate creation

1) To get top marks, you need to think of each poem as a **construct** that is **consciously created** by the **poet**.

2) This means that every **word** or **poetic technique** used in the poem is **deliberately chosen** by the poet and **affects** the poem's **meaning**.

3) To show the examiner that you understand this, you should write about **what** the **poet** does and **why**.

Focus on what the <u>poet</u> is doing. → Armitage uses the half-rhyme of "hurt" and "heart" to reflect the narrator's struggle to understand her husband's pain, which she can only partially grasp. ← Explain the effect of the poet's choice.

4) **Don't mix up** the **poet** and the **voice / narrator** of the poem — you need to show that the voice is a **construct** which **doesn't** necessarily **express** the poet's own **thoughts and feelings**.

5) Remember that poems are works of **imagination**, **not** straightforward **autobiography** — so be careful if you use **biographical details** about the poet as context.

6) However, it can be useful to consider how the **poet's background** might have **influenced** the poem. Think about the **ideas** and **attitudes** which shaped the poem's **creation**, **setting** or **reception**.

Analyse individual words and phrases

One way to impress the examiner is to comment on words or phrases that are rich in meaning. You need to really explore the meaning and effect of these examples. Here's how it's done:

In 'Valentine', the narrator asserts that the "fierce kiss" of the onion will linger on their lover's lips. Using the adjective "fierce" to describe the kiss gives the reader the impression of an intense love and passionate physical intimacy. However, the adjective also has connotations of aggression, implying that the relationship might be dangerous and possessive. By connecting the kiss to danger, Duffy suggests that there could be a tragic, painful side to the love in the poem. ← This example looks in detail at an individual word and analyses its effect.

Practice Questions

These Target Grade 8-9 questions are designed to help you stretch your knowledge, think about the poems in more depth and even see them in a new light — they're the perfect way to take your essays to the next level.

1) Compare how 'The Manhunt' and 'Mametz Wood' use images of brokenness and the effects that these images create.

2) 'The woman in 'She Walks in Beauty' is merely a blank canvas on which the speaker paints his own ideas of perfection.' Do you agree with this statement? Explain your answer.

3) 'The Romantic poets were often very critical of people in positions of authority.' Do you think 'London' and 'Ozymandias' support this statement?

4) 'The Soldier' and 'Sonnet 43' are both sonnets. In what ways do the poems conform to or subvert the expectations and traditions of the sonnet form?

5) 'Patriotism is a flawed value which damages lives.' How far do you think 'The Soldier' and 'Dulce et Decorum Est' support this statement?

6) 'Living Space' and the excerpt from 'The Prelude' each contain powerful descriptions of place. Which poem do you think describes place most effectively? Explain your answer.

7) Do you think 'As Imperceptibly as Grief' or 'A Wife in London' explores the experience of loss more effectively? Explain your answer.

8) 'In the past, women's experiences have been dictated largely by gender roles.' Do you think 'A Wife in London' and 'Afternoons' support this statement? Explain your answer.

9) 'Romantic love is about comfort and commitment.' To what extent do 'Cozy Apologia' and 'Valentine' support this statement? Explain your answer.

10) What do 'Death of a Naturalist' and 'Afternoons' suggest about how people change as they age? Which poem do you think portrays the effects of getting older most effectively?

11) 'An understanding of nature is vital to understanding human experience.' Discuss this statement with reference to 'Hawk Roosting' and 'To Autumn'.

Improve the Answer

The next couple of pages will give you a chance to practise your P.E.E.D. skills by adding quotes and developing the points in some sample answers. Enjoy...

You can find the answers for this section on p.92.

Complete this plan by adding quotes and developing points

1) Below is an exam question and a plan for answering it.

2) Find quotes from the poems to back up each of the language points in the table (marked A, B, C and D).

3) Make brief notes on your personal response to each poem (marked E and F) to complete the plan.

| 7 2 | In 'Death of a Naturalist', Heaney explores the theme of nature. Select one other poem from the anthology and compare the ways the poets present the natural world. |

	Death of a Naturalist	To Autumn
Themes and ideas	Childhood experiences of nature. Change.	Narrator admires the power of nature. Seasons pass.
Language	Sensory language ... **(A)**	Personification ... **(C)**
	Language of war ... **(B)**	Language of excess ... **(D)**
Form and Structure	Blank verse (unrhymed, steady rhythm). Enjambment.	Ode. Changing rhyme scheme. Structure reflects time passing.
Personal Response	**(E)**	**(F)**

Add quotes to improve these answers

In the sample answers below, replace each letter (A, B and C) with a suitable quote.

| 7 2 | In 'Dulce et Decorum Est', Owen explores ideas about conflict. Select one other poem from the anthology and compare the ways the poets present ideas about conflict. |

Answer Extract 1

'Dulce et Decorum Est' and 'The Manhunt' both use powerful imagery to show the physical suffering that conflict brings to those who have fought in war. In 'Dulce et Decorum Est', Owen uses the graphic imagery of the gas attack victim **(A)** to convey his suffering. In addition, the metaphor of the gas as a **(B)** emphasises its overwhelming nature. Similarly, in 'The Manhunt', the metaphor of **(C)** creates an emotive image of the man's broken body. By comparing the man to familiar physical objects, Armitage helps the reader to visualise the devastating consequences of war.

Answer Extract 2

Both Owen and Armitage use language to show the emotional toll that war can take on soldiers. The word **(A)** implies that the narrator is being slowly suffocated by his dreams. This idea could be a reference to the condition known then as 'shell shock', which caused severe emotional distress to many soldiers who had witnessed conflict. Similarly, in Armitage's poem, the narrator uses a metaphor to describe how the man has a **(B)**, which hints at deeply rooted emotional torment. Because his heart is now **(C)**, it is implied that he has lost some of his ability to love.

Improve the Answer

Have a go at developing these answers

1) Here are some **sample answers** to the question below.

2) In these extracts, the sentences followed by a letter (**A** or **B**) need to be **developed further**. Write an **extra sentence** to **develop** each point.

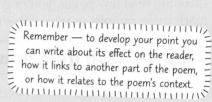

Remember — to develop your point you can write about its effect on the reader, how it links to another part of the poem, or how it relates to the poem's context.

---

7 2 Dharker explores feelings towards a place in 'Living Space'. Pick another poem from the anthology and compare the ways the poets explore feelings towards a place.

Answer Extract 1

The narrators of 'Living Space' and 'London' both use descriptions of a place to present inequality between classes. In Dharker's poem, the narrator describes Mumbai as a "slanted universe". The word "slanted" not only describes the sloping housing but also implies that something is not quite right — it could perhaps symbolise a wealth divide in the city. **(A)**. In contrast, in 'London', the narrator's emotive description of how a "sigh / Runs in blood down Palace walls" uses enjambment to mimic the trickling of blood. Here, the "Palace walls" form a boundary based on privilege, suggesting that the ruling classes shut themselves away from the city's suffering. **(B)**.

Answer Extract 2

Both poems use form to help illustrate each narrator's presentation of a place. In 'Living Space', the lines vary in length. Significantly, the line "The whole structure leans dangerously" is much longer than the others, and so reflects the building's precarious nature. **(A)**. However, 'London' has a much more rigid form. It follows a regular ABAB rhyme scheme and has a steady rhythm throughout. The consistency this creates reflects how the narrator perceives the suffering in London to be deeply ingrained in society. **(B)**.

Answer Extract 3

The narrators of 'Living Space' and 'London' present contrasting attitudes towards a place. In Dharker's poem, the first stanza ends with the word "miraculous", which is juxtaposed with the earlier, more chaotic, descriptions of the building to suggest the narrator is hopeful for those who live there. **(A)**. In contrast, the narrator of 'London' has a much more bleak outlook towards the city. His sense of hopelessness is conveyed when he describes "every cry of every Man", which uses repetition of "every" to suggest that the suffering is widespread. **(B)**.

Mark Scheme

Over the next few pages, you're going to put your examiner's hat on (I know, it's a dream come true) and mark some sample answers. This will help you to see what you need to do to get a great mark in your exam.

This section gets you to mark a range of sample answers

1) **Marking** sample exam answers is a **great way** to find out **exactly** what you need to do in the exam to get the grade you want.

2) Most of the answers in this section are only **extracts**, not **full answers**. The essays you'll write in the exam will be **longer** — more like the ones on pages 75-76 and 87-88.

3) The mark scheme below is **similar** to the one that the **examiners will use** to mark your exam answers.

4) Read the mark scheme **thoroughly** and make sure that you **understand everything**.

5) Once you **understand** the mark scheme, use it to mark the sample exam answers on the next few pages. Don't forget to **explain** why you chose each grade.

Use this mark scheme to mark the sample answers

Grade band	What is written
8-9	• Shows an insightful and critical analysis of the poem(s) Second part only — presents a critical comparison between the poems, discussing a wide range of similarities and/or differences • Effectively integrates a full range of precise examples to support interpretations • Closely analyses the use of language, structure and form, using technical terms effectively • Gives a detailed exploration of how the techniques used affect the reader • Convincingly explores original and alternative interpretations of the ideas, themes, attitudes and contexts of the poem(s)
6-7	• Shows a carefully thought out and developed analysis of the poem(s) Second part only — presents a focused comparison between the poems, clearly discussing their similarities and/or differences • Integrates well-chosen examples to support interpretations • Explores the use of language, structure and form, using correct technical terms • Examines the way the techniques used affect the reader • Gives careful consideration to the ideas, themes, attitudes and/or contexts of the poem(s), possibly offering some original interpretations
4-5	• Shows an understanding of the important aspects of the poem(s) Second part only — makes relevant comparisons between the poems, discussing their similarities and/or differences • Provides relevant examples to support interpretations • Explains the use of language, structure and form, using some relevant terms • Comments on how some of the techniques used affect the reader • Shows a clear understanding of the ideas, themes, attitudes and/or context of the poem(s)

You can also be awarded grades 1-3. We haven't included any sample answer extracts at 1-3 level though — so those grades aren't in this mark scheme.

Mark the Answer

Here's your first set of sample answers. For each one, think about where it fits in the mark scheme on page 84. Most answers won't fit the criteria for any one band exactly — it's about finding the best fit.

Have a go at marking these answer extracts

For each extract:

a) Write down the grade band (4-5, 6-7 or 8-9) you think the answer falls into.

b) Give at least two reasons why you chose that grade band.

> **7 1** Byron's narrator shows feelings of attraction in 'She Walks in Beauty'.
> Examine how Byron presents the feeling of attraction in the poem.

Answer Extract 1

Byron's use of contrasting images shows the narrator's appreciation for the woman's beauty. The images of "every raven tress" and the "nameless grace" that "softly lightens o'er her face" is an example of opposites — ravens are birds which are very dark, meaning it's unusual for this image to appear above a line with the word "lightens" in. Through contrasts like this, the narrator shows the reader his appreciation for the woman's beauty, as the opposites create the sense that he believes her beauty is perfectly balanced. Natural imagery, which Byron uses to compare her to the night, is a feature of Romantic poetry, which often looked at the relationship between nature and humans.

Answer Extract 2

The form of 'She Walks in Beauty' is used to emphasise the narrator's feeling of attraction. The rhyme scheme mimics the use of opposites related to light and dark which describe the woman's beauty; the repeating AB pattern mirrors the contrasting aspects of her appearance. The link between the poem's form and its meaning is further reinforced through the alternating use of enjambment and end-stopping in the first stanza and through the light, bouncy rhythm which conveys to the reader the effortlessness of the woman's beauty.

Answer Extract 3

Byron makes use of sound devices to present the narrator's feeling of attraction towards the subject of the poem. The alliteration of the 'cl' sound and the sibilance in the phrase "cloudless climes and starry skies" help to convey the idea of unification: Byron establishes pairings using the weather, skies, and light and dark, as well as repeated sounds. The poem as a whole is filled with pairings and antitheses, giving the reader the impression that the narrator is yearning to become part of a pair with the woman he desires. Moreover, the sibilance also creates a soft hissing sound, which could suggest a whisper or a gentle breeze. This gives the line an unreal, dreamlike quality, hinting to the reader that the woman is so attractive that she is otherworldly.

Mark the Answer

You must be getting the hang of this now — if you get much more practice you'll be putting those English examiners out of a job. Remember to look out for comparison of the two poems in these extracts.

Mark these answer extracts to a comparison question

For each extract:

a) Write down the grade band (4-5, 6-7 or 8-9) you think the answer falls into.

b) Give at least two reasons why you chose that grade band.

Remember to keep looking back at the mark scheme on page 84.

> **7 2**   Hardy presents the feeling of grief in 'A Wife in London'. Compare how grief is explored in this poem and in one other poem from the anthology.

Answer Extract 1

Both the wife in 'A Wife in London' and the narrator in 'As Imperceptibly as Grief' display signs of grief. The wife's grief is shown in the first half of Hardy's poem, after she learns that "He – has fallen – in the far South Land ..." The dashes and ellipsis here could imply that the wife is breaking down as she comes to the realisation that her husband has died. Similarly, in Dickinson's poem, a melancholy tone is established through the way "Summer lapsed away". While the wife in Hardy's poem may not have been accustomed to death (it's described as a "Tragedy"), Dickinson was perhaps more familiar with it, having lost several friends and relatives while she was still quite young — this could be why her narrator seems to handle loss better, and almost seems to find grief comforting.

Answer Extract 2

The grief in 'A Wife in London' creates a hopeless mood that runs throughout the poem, whereas the mood of Dickinson's poem lightens at the end. Hardy's poem ends in a bleak mood, because the husband's "hoped return" creates a sense of irony. By ending the poem in this way, the emotion of grief only becomes more intense as the poem progresses, as the reader also begins to share in the wife's grief. Dickinson's poem ends on the word "Beautiful", which contrasts with words with more negative meanings such as "harrowing" and "Perfidy" to suggest the narrator is more at ease than the wife in Hardy's poem and that her grief has come to an end.

Answer Extract 3

Both poets use aspects of form to give the reader an insight into the way each figure experiences grief. Hardy's poem follows an ABBAB rhyme scheme, in which the 'A' and 'B' rhymes could symbolise the relationship between the wife and her husband: the final 'B' rhyme is left alone without an 'A' rhyme to match it, just as the wife is left without a husband. The sense of incompleteness that this creates could reflect the incompleteness of the wife's life after her husband's death. The final 'B' rhyme feels unexpected, allowing the reader to share in the idea that death in war, and the sorrow it brings, also comes as a shock. In contrast, Dickinson's poem has one long stanza, which creates a sense of unbroken continuity to suggest that dealing with loss is a steady process. The use of dashes peters out as the poem progresses, further reflecting the way the narrator's sorrow eases gradually.

Mark the Answer

New page, new question and answer. Only this time it's the whole answer, not just an extract...

Now try marking this whole answer

> Make sure you've read the mark scheme on page 84.

a) Write down the grade band (4-5, 6-7 or 8-9) you think the answer falls into.

b) Give at least four reasons why you chose that grade band.

> | 7 | 1 | In 'Death of a Naturalist', Heaney gives a vivid presentation of the flax dam. Explore how Heaney presents the natural world in 'Death of a Naturalist'.

'Death of a Naturalist' comes from a collection of poems in which Heaney reflects on his childhood. Through the use of language with specific connotations, sound devices and form, Heaney effectively presents his retrospective appreciation of nature, but also how his perception of nature was changed by what he saw as he grew up. In this sense, 'Death of a Naturalist' can be seen as a poem that primarily explores the unappealing side of nature, but also how this side can be attractive to certain people. The conflicting feelings of interest and disgust explored in the poem reveal the fragility of the narrator's relationship with nature to the reader.

At the start of the poem, Heaney's narrator presents nature as unattractive and unappealing. Emotive verbs associated with decay, such as "festered" and "rotted", create a strong sense of the repulsive stench that the flax dam gave off. These words also establish the theme of death early on in the poem, which foreshadows the imminent metaphorical death of something else; it is hinted that the narrator's happiness when surrounded by nature will be short-lived. The theme of death is reinforced when the narrator remembers how "bluebottles / Wove a strong gauze of sound around the smell". This image uses sibilance to mimic the buzzing of the flies, while the fact that their "gauze" surrounds the smell suggests that death and decay (which are symbolised by the flies) are a crucial part of nature. The language of death also contrasts with what the reader might expect from poetry about nature, as poems about the natural world typically celebrate nature's ability to bring life, rather than take it away.

Nature is also shown to be menacing and dangerous. The personification of the "punishing sun" suggests that the sun is uncomfortably oppressive. The choice of the word "punishing" could reveal that the narrator has a childlike fear of being held to account for something they have done wrong; the reader later learns that this could be a punishment for 'stealing' the frogspawn. The narrator's fear of nature is heightened in the second stanza, in which the frogs are personified as "The great slime kings". This example uses language reminiscent of fairy tales to suggest that the narrator has entered an alternative reality in which the frogs are the rulers and the narrator is at their mercy. The onomatopoeia of the "slap" and "plop" creates a more threatening mood

This answer continues on page 88.

Mark the Answer

than the sound devices used in the first stanza, as the frogs' noises are described as "obscene threats", which contrasts with the way the rotting vegetation gargles "delicately" in line 5.

As the poem progresses, nature is increasingly presented in military terms, heightening the sense of threat it poses. The verb "Invaded" and the simile "Poised like mud grenades" present the frogs as soldiers or weapons, which reinforces the threatening mood, but also hints that the child's innocence has been lost. The collection that this poem comes from is generally considered to be autobiographical, so one interpretation of the extensive use of language of war could be that this is the voice of the older Heaney looking back on events that might have influenced his early life (such as the Second World War) and interpreting them from an adult perspective.

Despite the general presentation of nature as disgusting and threatening, in the first stanza the narrator reveals a childhood fascination with it. An example of this fascination is shown through the childlike voice in the long sentence in lines 15-19, which uses repetition of "and" in addition to childish language such as "mammy" to reflect how the narrator is captivated by nature. Additionally, the narrator's fascination extends to appreciating aspects of nature that others might not, as shown in the phrase "warm thick slobber / Of frogspawn that grew like clotted water", which uses assonance of the 'o' and 'or' sounds to emphasise how sticky the frogspawn becomes. Although the older narrator sees the frogs as disgusting, the frogspawn's warmth, added to the way it is described as "slobber" (which brings to mind a dog), suggests that as a child, he viewed it as a pet which could offer comfort and companionship.

Through the abrupt change in the narrator's attitude, Heaney presents his relationship with nature as fragile. This is shown through the volta "In rain." in line 21, which sounds serious and breaks away from the longer lines expressing delight earlier in the stanza. This suggests that the narrator's shift from viewing nature enthusiastically to being repulsed by it was also sudden. Because the poem is structured so that the child's perspective gives way to the older narrator's more dominant voice, Heaney could be suggesting that once that childish fascination with nature has been lost, it can be remembered, but not readopted. In this sense, the poem could be interpreted as an appeal encouraging younger readers to cherish their relationships with nature.

Heaney gives an effective and detailed presentation of nature using emotive imagery, sound devices and aspects of form and structure, all of which make the description of the flax dam highly evocative and accessible to the reader. By establishing nature as unappealing from early on, Heaney is able to emphasise the narrator's childhood fascination with it, as well as his later disgust. Because the poem is retrospective and ends on a feeling of uncertainty, the reader is left with the sense that the narrator cannot regain his positive relationship with nature; the metaphorical 'death' of the 'naturalist' is in fact as permanent as it's suggested to be in the poem's title.

Glossary

alliteration	Where words that are close together **start** with the same sound, e.g. "**w**innowing **w**ind".
ambiguity	Where a word or phrase has **two or more** possible **interpretations**.
anaphora	Where a word or phrase is **repeated** at the **start** of **consecutive sentences** or **lines**.
antithesis	Where the **contrast** between **two ideas** is emphasised by using a **repeated structure**, e.g. "One shade the more, one ray the less".
autobiographical	Describing something that happened in the **poet's life**.
blank verse	Poetry written in iambic pentameter that **doesn't rhyme**.
caesura (plural caesurae)	A **pause** in a line of poetry, e.g. the semi-colon in "'Tis the morrow; the fog hangs thicker".
cliché	A **stereotypical** phrase or idea that is **overused**, e.g. a "red rose" to represent love.
colloquial	Sounding like everyday **spoken** language, e.g. "They all had sissy names".
connotations	The **suggestions** that words can make **beyond** their obvious meaning.
consonance	**Repetition** of a **consonant sound** in nearby words, e.g. "full-grown lambs loud bleat".
direct address	When the narrator **speaks directly** to the reader or another character, e.g. "I give you an onion".
dramatic monologue	A **form** of poetry that uses the assumed voice of a **single speaker** who is **not the poet** to address an **implied audience**, e.g. 'Hawk Roosting'.
ellipsis	A set of three dots which can give the impression of an unfinished thought or of missing details.
emotive	Something that makes you **feel** a particular **emotion**.
end-stopping	Finishing a line of poetry with the **end** of a **phrase or sentence**.
enjambment	When a sentence or phrase runs over from **one line** or **stanza** to the **next**.
euphemism	When a deliberately **vague** word or phrase is used in order to **avoid** saying something **unpleasant**.
figurative language	Language that is used in a **non-literal** way to create an effect, e.g. personification.
first person	When a poet writes about themselves or their group, using words like "**I**", "**my**", "**we**" and "**our**".
foreshadowing	Where the poet **hints** at an **event to come** earlier on in the poem.
form	The **type** of poem, e.g. a sonnet or an ode, and its **features**, like number of lines, rhyme and rhythm.
free verse	Poetry that **doesn't rhyme** and has **no regular rhythm** or **line length**.
half-rhymes	Words that have a **similar**, but not identical, **end sound**. E.g. "hurt" and "heart" in 'The Manhunt'.
hyperbole	The use of **exaggeration** to **emphasise** a point.
iambic pentameter	Poetry with a **metre** of **ten syllables** — five of them stressed, and five unstressed. The **stress** falls on **every second syllable**, e.g. "To swell the gourd, and plump the hazel shells".
iambic tetrameter	Like iambic pentameter but with a metre of **eight** syllables — four stressed and four unstressed. E.g. "A heart whose love is innocent!"
imagery	Language that creates a **picture in your mind**. It includes **metaphors**, **similes** and **personification**.
irony	When **words** are used to **imply the opposite** of what they normally mean. It can also mean when there is a difference between **what people expect** and **what actually happens**.
juxtaposition	When a poet puts two ideas, events, characters or descriptions **close to each other** to encourage the reader to **contrast** them, e.g. Blake juxtaposes happiness and death in "Marriage hearse".

Glossary

Glossary

language	The **choice of words** used. Different kinds of language have **different effects**.
metaphor	A way of describing something by saying that it **is something else**, e.g. the "unexploded mine" in the soldier's mind in 'The Manhunt'. An **extended metaphor** is a metaphor that is **carried on**.
metre	The arrangement of stressed and unstressed syllables to create **rhythm** in a line of poetry.
monosyllables	Words with only **one syllable**, e.g. "I sit in the top of the wood, my eyes closed".
mood	The **feel** or **atmosphere** of a poem, e.g. humorous, threatening, eerie.
narrative	Writing that tells a **story**, e.g. 'Ozymandias'.
narrator	The **person** speaking the words. E.g. the narrator of 'The Manhunt' is an injured soldier's wife.
ode	A poem written in **praise** of a person or thing.
onomatopoeia	A word that **sounds like** the thing it's describing, e.g. "bleat" and "twitter" in 'To Autumn'.
oxymoron	A phrase which appears to **contradict** itself, e.g. "harrowing Grace".
personification	Describing a non-living thing as if it has **human qualities** and **feelings**, or **behaves** in a human way, e.g. "A dust whom England bore, shaped, made aware".
Petrarchan sonnet	A form of **sonnet** in which the first eight lines have a regular ABBA rhyme scheme and often **introduce** a problem, while the final six lines have a different rhyme scheme and **solve** the problem.
plosive	A **short burst of sound** made when you say a word containing the letters b, d, g, k, p or t.
rhetoric	Language used by the poet to **persuade** you of a particular view.
rhetorical question	A **question** that doesn't need an answer, but is asked to **make** or **emphasise** a point.
rhyme scheme	A **pattern** of rhyming words in a poem. E.g. 'London' has an **ABAB** rhyme scheme — this means that the **first** and **third** lines in each stanza rhyme, and so do the **second** and **fourth** lines.
rhyming couplet	A **pair of rhyming lines** that are next to each other, e.g. the first two lines of 'Cozy Apologia'.
rhythm	A **pattern of sounds** created by the arrangement of **stressed** and **unstressed** syllables.
sensory language	Language that appeals to any of the **five senses**, e.g. "hear, at every jolt, the blood / Come gargling".
sibilance	Repetition of 's' and 'sh' sounds, e.g. "**sh**od with **s**teel, / We hi**ss**'d along the poli**sh**'d i**c**e".
simile	A way of describing something by **comparing** it to something else, usually by using the words "like" or "as", e.g. "their loose necks pulsed like sails".
sonnet	A form of poem with **fourteen lines** that usually follows a **clear rhyme scheme**.
stanza	A **group of lines** in a poem.
structure	The **order** and **arrangement** of ideas and events in a poem, e.g. how it begins, develops and ends.
syllable	A single **unit of sound** within a word. E.g. "all" has one syllable, "always" has two.
symbolism	When an object **stands for something else**. E.g. the statue of Ozymandias symbolises human power, and the eggs in 'Living Space' symbolise new life and hope.
third person	When a poet writes about a character who **isn't** the speaker, using words like "**he**" or "**she**".
tone	The **mood** or **feelings** suggested by the way the narrator **writes**, e.g. bitter, reflective.
voice	The **characteristics** of the **person** narrating the poem. Poems are usually written either using the poet's voice, as if they're speaking to you **directly**, or the voice of a **character**.
volta	A **turning point** in a poem, when the argument or tone **changes dramatically**.

Glossary

Index

Answers

These are the answers to the exercises in Section Six. They're only suggestions, so don't worry if what you've written doesn't match exactly — there are lots of possible answers.

Page 82 — Improve the Answer

Sample Plan

(A) "frogspawn that grew like clotted water"

(B) "Poised like mud grenades"

(C) "Close bosom-friend of the maturing sun"

(D) "fill all fruit with ripeness to the core"

(E) Although the frogspawn sounds unappealing to the reader, it still fascinates the child narrator. However, the increasing use of military language suggests the older voice is more fearful of nature.

(F) Personifying autumn gives the season an active role, making the reader more appreciative of the bountiful harvest it produces.

Answer Extract 1

(A) "flound'ring like a man in fire or lime"

(B) "green sea"

(C) "the rungs of his broken ribs"

Answer Extract 2

(A) "smothering"

(B) "sweating, unexploded mine / buried deep in his mind"

(C) "grazed"

Page 83 — Improve the Answer

Answer Extract 1

(A) This could relate to how the majority of people in Mumbai, where the poem is set, live in slums that are overshadowed by the high-rise towers inhabited by much wealthier people.

(B) By using such emotive imagery, Blake could have been trying to instil a passionate desire for revolution in readers at the time.

Answer Extract 2

(A) The poem's varied line lengths also create a sense of unpredictability, encouraging the reader to think about how uncertain the inhabitants' lives are.

(B) Furthermore, Blake's use of the first person makes the poem feel personal and creates a strong impression of what the city is truly like.

Answer Extract 3

(A) This sense of hope is reinforced through the image of the "eggs in a wire basket", as eggs are often regarded as symbols for new life.

(B) Here, Blake subverts the expectation that men should be emotionally strong to emphasise how the suffering is unrelenting and indiscriminate.

Page 85 — Mark the Answer

Answer Extract 1

I think this answer would get a grade 4-5 because it makes a point supported with quotes from the poem, as well as showing a clear understanding of the poem's context. To get a higher grade it needs to explain the effect of the quotes in more detail.

Answer Extract 2

I would give this answer a grade 6-7 because it gives a thoughtful analysis of the poet's use of form and uses the correct technical vocabulary. However, some ideas need developing further.

Answer Extract 3

I think this answer would get a grade 8-9. It gives a perceptive and original analysis, using precise examples and technical terms. It also gives an insightful exploration of how the poet's techniques affect the reader.

Page 86 — Mark the Answer

Answer Extract 1

I would give this extract a grade 6-7 because it makes a point, gives examples from the texts and considers the context in which Dickinson's poem was written. To get a higher grade, the effects the examples create need to be explained in more detail.

Answer Extract 2

I think this answer would get a grade 4-5. This is because it makes points about the poems' moods and structures and backs them up with examples that are briefly explained. To get a higher grade it needs to actually analyse the examples — it's too descriptive at the moment.

Answer Extract 3

I think this answer would get a grade 8-9 because it gives an insightful analysis of the poems' forms using examples that are explained effectively. It also explores the effect on the reader in detail.

Pages 87-88 — Mark the Answer

I think this answer should be awarded a grade 8-9 because it makes a detailed and critical analysis of the poem and focuses on the effects of form, structure and language on the reader. It also makes relevant references to context, uses a wide range of technical vocabulary, and gives well-explained examples of the poet's techniques.

AWHR42